SHEPHERDING GOD'S FLOCK **3**

Pastoral Leadership

JAY E. ADAMS

BAKER BOOK HOUSE
Grand Rapids, Michigan

PHOTOLITHOPRINTED BY CUSHING - MALLOY, INC.
ANN ARBOR, MICHIGAN, UNITED STATES OF AMERICA
1978

CONTENTS

PREFACE

With the completion of this third volume, I plan to pause for a time before resuming work on the remaining volumes in this series. I have made this decision since there are several other books pending that are closer to the front of the line. Lord willing, I shall begin to write the last two or three volumes in about a year or two and, hopefully, at that time I shall pursue the project to its fulfillment. Yet to consider in those future volumes are such subjects as liturgics, worship, the celebration of the sacraments, weddings, funerals, church discipline, the protection of the flock from unbelief, heresy, cults and divisiveness, and presbyterial, denominational and extra-congregational ministry. All of these areas are of significance, and most of them have received but scanty treatment by conservative writers. Therefore, I urge you to help me by your prayers to conclude the writing that now lies at hand with dispatch, in order that I may take up the work where I now must leave off. The final volume in the series will carry an index to the whole.

Jay Adams
Professor of Practical Theology
Westminster Theological Seminary
Chestnut Hill, Pennsylvania
1975

INTRODUCTION

Many Christian ministers who believe the Scriptures to be the inspired Word of God and who are concerned about serving Jesus Christ as fruitfully as possible nevertheless seem to have a strange blind spot when it comes to serving Him through Church administration. Some go so far as to decry planning, organization and management as "dependence upon the arm of flesh," while others see it as a wearisome necessity and go plodding along under the sagging weight of a burden that they must carry as "the cross that a minister must bear," or "the price he must pay to be able to preach the gospel."

Certainly for every minister who thoroughly enjoys the work of administration (and there are *some* who get themselves so involved in it that everything else suffers including preaching and pastoral care) there are dozens who can be heard any month at the local ministerium crying the blues over the intolerable load that such work demands. Some call church management a waste of time; others see it as a necessary evil. Many resent the time that it requires which keeps them from the "real work" of the ministry. Yet, in the New Testament, proven managerial ability[1] is set forth prominently as a crucial qualification for the selection of an overseer.[2] Without this ability, Paul says, a minister cannot properly carry out the "work of an overseer" (which includes "taking managerial care of the church of God"). From this verse we can see (1) that management gifts and skills are necessary for discharging the ministerial duties enjoined by God (he must be able to "manage well"), (2) that management is a necessary part of such duties (it is part of overseeing "work," v.1), and (3) that the church suffers when such management fails to be forthcoming (the church needs managerial "care," v.5).

To think, therefore, of planning and church administration as dependence upon worldly or fleshly means is to think in categories not only

---

[1] *Proistemi*—literally "presiding over."
[2] 1 Timothy 3:1-5 (especially vv. 4,5). Indeed the word *episcopos* ("overseer") itself indicates that the work of administration is inherent in the ministerial office. The word "overseer" might as readily be translated "manager" or "superintendent."

foreign, but entirely antithetical to the Bible. While church administration *may* degenerate into fleshly dependence upon worldly ways and means, this is in no way a necessary consequence. Indeed, one of the most worldly and unchristian ways of dishonoring God is by the careless, sloppy, confused and confusing manner in which some try to carry on His work. Anything, pursued in an unbiblical manner, anything not Spirit-controlled, will become fleshly — whether tightly organized and managed well, or whether loosely thrown together. The Spirit is neither bound by organization, as some think ("We must not plan since this may hinder the Spirit"), nor is He unable to work in freer contexts ("Until we work out all of the arrangements we cannot expect God to move"). He sovereignly works when and where and how *He* pleases. We do not have to "free things up" as some maintain (possibly as an excuse for failure to organize). While He may choose to break out beyond our plans and programs, the Spirit thereby does not call us to abandon or to become careless about planning and leadership. When we not only plan, but also submit our plans to the Spirit for His blue-penciling, we do well.[3] We must remember that all that the Scriptures say about the necessity for good leadership (and they say *much* about it) was inspired by the Holy Spirit Himself. It is of utmost necessity, therefore, to recognize at the outset that good leadership, planning and management in the Church of Christ is not merely tolerated or permitted (as one might suppose from listening to many ministers) but is required and encouraged by the Holy Spirit. To put it tersely: biblical administration is spiritual.

If the last sentence in the preceding paragraph is true, then ministers dare not speak of administration as a waste of time, or carnal, or of less importance than the other work to which they are called. It is no less spiritual to plan a series of meetings well so that the gospel may be preached than to do the preaching. The one is a vital means for facilitating the other. Indeed, leadership among the people of God, as one may see by reading either the book of Judges or the book of Acts, is Spirit motivated. It cannot be denied that the Holy Spirit freely uses human leadership, guided by His Word, as the principal means of achieving His purposes. Spiritual leadership is leadership that He empowers to carry on His work.

Nor must leadership, planning and administration be set off from the "real work." This false disjunction has done much harm. Planning, for instance, *is* the real work of the overseer. Indeed, it is so bound up with

---

[3]Cf. James 4:13-17. N. B., James does not *forbid* planning; rather his main concern is to *show how to plan*—by conditioning every plan through a willingness to have God revise or overturn it ("say, 'If the Lord wills. . .' ").

preaching, with evangelism and with pastoral care that it can never be separated from them. The two sides go together. Leadership *is* a part of the work; planning *is* a part of the work; management *is* a part of the work of the minister. If that work is biblical, and Spirit-motivated, it is spiritual work. And, far from hampering the proclamation of the gospel, such work becomes the vehicle that facilitates it. The two go together so closely that, ordinarily, under normal conditions, there will be little or no successful preaching, evangelism or counseling without proper planning, structure and leadership.[4]

In this matter, much depends upon one's viewpoint. Since wrong attitudes quickly grow from wrong orientations let us take a hard look at this question from another angle for a moment.

A general does not consider his army to be a liability, but rather the principal asset that he has for winning the war. Because he clearly recognizes that without a well organized army he can do nothing to achieve the goals and purposes for which his generalship exists, he prizes his army. He sees to it that every unit is well disciplined. He sets up networks of rapid communication. He wants not only every division but every soldier in it to be fully skilled and equipped for every task to which he is called. He is deeply involved not only in strategy and command but in organizing a body that will know what to do and how to do it when he determines the proper actions and issues a command.

Why must he be concerned with all of these matters? Because they all hang together; each is dependent upon the other. The general knows that he cannot fight his battles alone. He knows the importance of clear communication, the necessity for training and how essential good discipline is. It is precisely because he is intensely aware that the work to which he has been called must be done *by means of his army* that he busies himself with such matters. It may be said, therefore, that the professional viewpoint of a good general is army-oriented rather than self-oriented. He has come to recognize that just as his soldiers in many ways must depend upon his leadership, he too must depend upon his army; and that means that he will see to it that it becomes a body that is well trained, well organized, etc. In short, since he must depend upon his army, he must endeavor to make his army *dependable*.

The bad attitude of many pastors toward administration stems from a faulty viewpoint and a defective vocational orientation. They complain about their congregations, but they have done little to make them

---

[4]Cf. Jay Adams, *Your Place in the Counseling Revolution* (Presbyterian and Reformed Publishing Co., Nutley: 1975), pp. 40ff.

dependable. This attitude surfaces in words and phrases that (although not always expressed quite so boldly) amount to saying: "I can do the Lord's work *without* my congregation" or "If they won't work with me, then so much the worse for them; I'll do it alone."

This viewpoint needs correction in several particulars. Principally, it fails to distinguish between the pastor's obligations before God as an individual Christian and his work *as a shepherd.* As an individual, in some extreme situations it may be possible to continue to serve Christ even when others refuse.[5] But, *as a shepherd,* what can he do without sheep?

An attitude of independence toward the flock is virtual rebellion against the Chief Shepherd; it amounts to a resignation from the task to which Christ called him. Instead, a minister must come to see that his designated task is in its entirety *sheep oriented..* The great Shepherd of the sheep did not call him to some abstract work called "shepherding"; but to the actual earthy task of working with wandering, sick, wounded, smelly sheep. Shepherding is always concrete. That is to say, it involves all of the problems of caring for *sheep.*

And, as is the case with the general, the sort of shepherding to which he is called goes beyond merely tending and feeding the flock for its own benefit. The Chief Shepherd of His sheep wants his undershepherds to nourish, train, mobilize and deploy the flock in ways that *serve* Him and bring honor to His Name. That is to say, the shepherd becomes sheep oriented in his work because he is already Shepherd oriented in his allegience. It is out of love for Him that he serves among His flocks.

As every general knows, it is his task not merely to care for his troops, as an end in itself. His work includes seeing to their welfare and effectiveness *so that they will be ready and able to serve his country.* So too, a good undershepherd recognizes that shepherding is *for a purpose.* He readies and organizes the flock so that the sheep may be able to follow his leadership in fighting the battles of the Lord. The flock, like the army, is the principal vehicle by which the Lord has chosen to carry out His purposes and by which He spreads His glory in the world. Therefore, every pastor must become deeply *commited* to the task of organizing, equipping and leading a well-disciplined flock of God's people in Christ's service. He must become committed to it as a *spiritual* task. When he is so committed, he will not look upon church management as a dull, burdensome and necessary evil, but rather as a vital, exciting and challenging part of the total task for which he has been chosen by Christ.

---

[5]However, no one may dare declare himself independent of Christ's Church (cf. Hebrews 10:25). Also, he must remember, there always are others who have not bowed the knee to Baal.

In the first chapter, therefore, we shall turn our attention to some of the biblical data that show the place and importance of administrative tasks.

CHAPTER ONE
SHEPHERDS LEAD

To begin with, let me point out that the Scriptures consistently refer to shepherds as "leaders." In one sense, leading may be thought of as the whole task that comprises such matters as training, administration, organization, guidance, motivation, etc. In another sense, it may be narrowed to mean *guidance by example.* I am not going to try to distinguish between the various senses in which leadership may be viewed since the Scriptures themselves seem not to make any such hard-and-fast distinctions. As a matter of fact, the Scriptures seem not to distinguish sharply between any of the functions of shepherdly work. Rather, they view the work holistically even when speaking about its various aspects. Sometimes they use one term and sometimes another to describe the various functions that a shepherd performs in the tending of a flock. It would be unwise, therefore, to try to sharpen the focus too greatly. Instead, I shall simply note what sorts of tasks biblical leadership involves. Perhaps in that way we may be able to develop a view of Shepherdly leadership that distinguishes but does not separate functions which of necessity seem to overlap. The essential fact to grasp is that any attempts to lead sheep that ignore, minimize or purposely eliminate any of the several facets of leadership that are scripturally discernible, thereby weaken and dilute both the biblical concept and the actual ministering power of those who make these attempts. In the passages to which I shall make reference in the paragraphs that follow, one can see at least these elements: responsibility, planning, organization, guidance, and example.

The Shepherd as Participant

Notice that when the Scriptures call shepherds "leaders" they continually picture them as *participants* in the activities into which they lead their sheep. They are never looked upon as armchair theorists, but rather as themselves down there on the plain, up there in the mountains, travelling the paths trod by the sheep themselves. Shepherdly leadership is concrete, participative, involved leadership. Shepherds are *with* the sheep; keeping watch over their flocks by night, passing through the valleys where in every shadow lurks the possibility of death from a wild animal, gently leading those with young and gathering the lambs (cf. especially Isaiah 40:11; Ezekiel 34:15; Psalm 23). It is the shepherd who "leads them out" of the fold and who "goes before them" (John 10:3,4). He defends them from the wolf with his rod. No wonder they are called simply, but pregnantly, "leaders" in Hebrews 13:7,17,24. That is why the writer may urge the sheep to consider their way of life and to imitate their faith (v.7). The shepherd is an involved example.

The Shepherd as Organizer

It is essential for a proper understanding of this leadership to notice what happens when there is no leadership or faulty leadership. Again and again we are told that as the result of such conditions the sheep are "scattered"[1] (e.g., Ezekiel 34:5). Without leadership, the sheep become confused, each turns to "his own way," and "wanders off." That is why Zechariah was able to portray the disorder among the disciples that accompanied the death of Christ so vividly by use of this shepherdly figure when he prophesied: "Smite the shepherd and the sheep will scatter" (Zechariah 13:7). Indeed, the biblical phrase "as sheep without a shepherd" has become proverbial. Yet like most familiar sayings, we take it for granted and we seldom think of what is means. Consider, for a moment, something of its import. Sheep are helpless and prone to scatter; i.e., to break up into separate single units, to become disorganized and to disintegrate *as a flock*. Unlike "birds of a feather" that "flock together," sheep do not of themselves tend to do so. It is shepherding that produces flocking among sheep. Flocking, or the organization of individual sheep into a definable entity called a flock, is a principal activity of a shepherd. By faithful, personal leadership that involves responsible participation on his part such congregational organization is accomplished. Shepherdly leadership, then, has as one of its chief ends to bring about cohesion and *order*.

The Shepherd as Planner

But notice too, sheep, even where there is a good shepherd, tend to "go astray," i.e., as Isaiah put it, they are prone to turn, "each one to his own way" (Isaiah 53:6). There is, then, a second feature closely related to disorganization. The idea of *wandering* also is prominent (cf. Ezekiel 34:6 and Zechariah 10:2). Sheep not only scatter individually, but as a result

---

[1] *Putz* = scattering, dispersion and confusion. All three ideas are inherent in the word.

wander aimlessly in their own way.[2] It is the Shepherd's work to turn aimless wandering into purposeful travel leading at length to the still waters and to the green pastures. The sheep on his own heads aimlessly in any direction without thought for where he is going or for what the consequence of such a course may be. He thereby exposes himself to grave dangers (Ezekiel 34:8). But the Chief Shepherd is concerned to guide His sheep in the "paths of righteousness." Indeed, in that great covenantal passage where the sacrificial Lamb of God Himself becomes the Shepherd, He guides His martyrs "to springs of the water of life" (Revelation 7:17). So, just as flocking is a shepherdly activity that overcomes the sheep's tendency to scatter by bringing order and cohesion, so too *leading toward a destination* (green grass, still waters) is a shepherdly activity aimed at overcoming proneness to wander by setting forth goals and objectives for the flock. These two activities — organization and biblical goal setting — are so fundamental to shepherdly leadership that they run through every phase of it.

The Shepherd as Ruler

Let us also notice how frequently God calls the minister a "ruler" or "manager," revealing a slightly different facet of shepherdly work. The word *proistemi* ("to preside over, to manage") occurs not only in I Timothy 3:4,5 where proven ability at managerial rule is designated as a requirement for a minister, but also in such passages as I Timothy 5:17; Romans 12:8 and I Thessalonians 5:12. Shepherdly leaders, according to Hebrews 13:17, must be "obeyed." Shepherds were "rulers"; indeed, the thought moves in both directions—kings and other rulers in the Old Testament were often called "shepherds." (Cf. Jeremiah 23, and especially, the remarkable Cyrus prophecy in Isaiah 44:28.) The two concepts are *fused* as God in the second Psalm speaking of Christ declares: "You shall rule (literally, "shepherd") them with a rod of iron."[3] This great prophecy is picked up in Revelation

---

[2]The story of the Book of Judges is the story of wandering sheep without a shepherd. Whenever there was no leadership, every man did what was right in his own eyes (Judges 17:6). When God sent judges to lead, the people followed in the ways of God. Cf. also Deuteronomy 12:8.

[3]The Hebrew of Psalm 2:9 reads "You shall smash them with an iron bar." A slight change in the pointing of the original text leads to the LXX rendering which agrees with the usage in Revelation. From the ironical play on words used in Micah 7:14 "Shepherd. . . with a rod," there is reason to see here a growingly close association. So that G. B. Caird, *et al,* have far less warrant for saying that the LXX and John "made a mistake" in thus rendering the word by *poimaneis* (shepherd) than one at first might think. It is likely that the two words—close in sound—had come to be used interchangeably whenever speaking of a forced rule. In smashing the rule of the kings (v. 3) by the missionary preaching of the church (Revelation 19:5), Christ began his rule over the nations (cf. Jay Adams, *The Time Is At Hand,* pp. 80ff.).

2:26,27; 12:5 and 19:15 where in its application the (probably intended) ambiguity also remains.

Of greatest importance is that in all of this, the *leading* work of the Chief and Great Shepherd of the sheep is reflected. It is *God* who *"leads* Joseph as a flock" (Psalm 80:1; also Psalm 23; John 10), who organizes both Jew and Gentile into one flock, who seeks the lost sheep, and who "rules" with the rod of iron.

Shepherdly leadership, then, is responsible participant exemplary leadership that involves:

(1) *Planning* (i.e., the setting of goals and of objectives for the progress of the flock as it seeks to honor God in all of its activities and endeavors; determining where the green grass grows and the still waters lie, and how to discover and guide the sheep into the paths of righteousness that lead there).

(2) *Organization* (i.e., flocking; bringing sheep *together* as a flock, or congregation, teaching and helping them to live, learn, love, and labor together for Jesus Christ).

(3) *Rule* (i.e., the authoritative instruction in and application of the Word of God to the individual and corporate activities of the sheep; management). Other elements either may be distinguished from or subsumed under these, but shepherdly leadership at least always involves these three.

EXERCISE

For the Student

Interview your own pastor (or some other pastor) briefly:
1. To discover his views on pastoral leadership (jot these down, take them on cassette, etc.) and be prepared to share and discuss these with the class.
2. To let him know that you are taking this course, and to ask him if he would be willing to work with you in a variety of ways in the weeks ahead (you might show him some of the assignments in this book that may require pastoral help).

For the Pastor

1. Consider your own attitude toward leadership. Is it
   good   ☐
   poor   ☐
   inadequate ☐

2. Rate your abilities and performance with reference to:

	good	poor	inadequate
leadership responsibility	☐	☐	☐
planning	☐	☐	☐
organization	☐	☐	☐
guidance	☐	☐	☐
example	☐	☐	☐

3. In the space below, write out suggestions for improvement.

CHAPTER TWO
LEADERSHIP IN THE CHURCH

All of the leadership activities of the Christian shepherd occur within a given organizational framework: the visible church of the Lord Jesus Christ. While there is plenty of room for individualization by congregations, and for the use of personal gifts among the members of those congregations, nevertheless all such variety occurs within a basic, given structure ordained, built and maintained by Christ Himself. That Church is an organic entity that manifests itself in this world through a visible structure that, for its maintenance, requires planning, organization and rule.

The shepherd must see this Church organization not as an impediment to the smooth functioning of the Church itself, but — as it was intended to be — the very vehicle through which shepherdly work for individuals and families as well as for the whole flock may be carried on. The organized Church is not an evil to be put up with, as some seem to think, but rather the visible manifestation of the body of Christ.

Because it has a visible, organized structure, the Church must be *managed* (I Timothy 3:4,5). And Christ has given officers in the Church to carry out these managerial functions (cf. Ephesians 4:11,12).

Mismanagement, not organization, actually is the evil that so often constitutes the underlying difficulty. It is not easy to bring sinners together into one flock and to maintain the unity and peace of that flock while carrying out the orders of the Chief Shepherd to walk through the barren shadowy valleys toward the grassy pastures that He has mapped out. Not only mismanagement but discouragement, weariness and fear can get in the way. Such work calls for organized guidance through little known paths (that sometimes the sheep do not want to take) toward clear objectives; that is to say, the work calls for good management. Management is responsible, authoritative, organizational leadership.

Let us therefore take a closer look at the authority structure of this flock over which Christ, the Chief Shepherd (I Peter 5:4) through His undershepherds, is the "Shepherd and Overseer" (I Peter 2:25). I shall not limit my discussion to shepherdly images alone, rich as these may be, but shall range over several of the figures of speech used to delineate and delimit the organizational structure of Christ's Church.

Unlike the sort of hierarchical situation that exists in business and in many other organizations, the Church of Jesus Christ is *His* Flock over which He rules both directly and through undershepherds. The rulers of His flock, as well as those whom they rule, all take orders directly from Him. But these leaders are not legislators. He as the Chief Shepherd has appointed leaders and has given to them *His* authority to lead and to manage the flock. This authority is great, yet limited; and it is entirely delegated. No authority exists within the Church except His own.

To each member of the flock, Christ has given gifts through His Spirit and has assigned them tasks to do that are appropriate to those gifts.[1] He has provided leadership for the purpose of helping every sheep to discover, develop and deploy his gifts in ways that contribute to the welfare of the entire flock and that further His purposes in this world.[2] And in accordance with the abilities granted and the leadership requisite for their proper exercise, He has given each member authority to minister in His name.[3] All tasks must be carried out for the honor of the Chief Shepherd. It is clear, therefore, that all leadership in the Church is *functional*. None exists for one's own ends, nor for his personal aggrandizement.

Each sheep in the flock must respect and submit to the authority of Christ, and must recognize that all authority that is exercised legitimately within the flock is His authority. There is no lesser authority. Therefore, he must submit to the undershepherds who manage and exercise oversight as he would submit to Christ Himself so long as they speak in accordance with the Scriptures (cf. Hebrews 13:17). Ultimately each sheep, therefore, submits to Christ alone for it is *He* who is the Shepherd, and they are *His* sheep.

In submitting to the care and discipline of the Church he does so "in the Lord." That is to say, he belongs to a kingdom (to change the figure) that is a constitutional monarchy. It differs, however, from other such monarchies in that the constitution was imposed by the Monarch Himself, not for His own instruction, limitation, etc., but so that every member of the body politic might know the laws and ordinances that He has ordained. By this constitution they may judge the actions and the commands even of

---

[1]Cf. *The Christian Counselor's Manual,* pp. 344-347. See also *infra,* ch. 10.
[2]Ephesians 4:11-16.
[3]Revelation 1:6.

the leaders. While allegiance is to Christ alone, the terms of that allegiance are set forth in the Scriptures. He alone laid down these terms; they have not been acquired through legislation devised by the leadership.

The constitution of the kingdom therefore is not a civil or social contract, negotiated and finally agreed upon by its members after compromises and trade-offs. The Church is neither a democracy nor a republic; it is a theocracy. The Bible is a covenant document divinely revealed and deposited with the Church by the Sovereign Himself. In it are the principles of management that the Sovereign has imposed upon His subjects. The authority of the leadership, individually and corporately, everywhere is conditioned by this constitution, by which also their exercise of Christ's authority is enjoined and delimited. The task of the leadership within the Church, therefore, is to declare, to minister and to administrate. There is no power to legislate.

Every member within the flock must grant to the leadership all proper deference and great respect,[4] but at the same time Christ has made each member responsible to exercise individual judgment concerning the leadership that he follows. That means that the leaders must teach each member adequately enough that he may judge whether those things that they command are truly in accord with the constitution (cf. especially the powerful word of the Apostle Paul on this question in Acts 17:11).

Yet, if a member disagrees with the decisions of the leadership, and because of conscience before God finds that he must refuse to submit to the orders that they give, he must do even that submissively (i.e., in a proper spirit that acknowledges the position and authority that Christ has granted to the leaders of His Church). Moreover, he must recognize the grave danger in which he may be placing himself by such a refusal. It is possible otherwise that:

1. He may be found to be opposing Christ Himself.
2. He may be showing disrespect for Christ, by disregarding the authority that He invested in His officers (cf. I Thessalonians 5:12,13, NASV).

Because of these dangers, only after great care and willingness to be taught and corrected by the leadership as they explain the Word of God to him, may he refuse to submit to them. And then may he do so only if he is thoroughly convinced of their failure to base their case upon the Scriptures. He may not refuse to submit to authority because of personal differences or

---

[4]Cf. Hebrews 13:7,17; I Thessalonians 5:12,13. The respect enjoined in these passages is of the highest level.

because of conflicts of any other sort. He must remember always that the authority to which he submits is not theirs but rather is the authority of Christ. And pastors, difficult as it may seem to them, must teach this submission to their members. Too many congregations have been split because members had not the foggiest notion that such submission is required by God.

Even in those rare instances in which he may find himself basically at odds with the leadership of the Church, a member must be careful about the *manner* in which he differs. He may not do so in a rebellious or independent spirit. Such differences must be stated in a spirit of sorrow and with a willingness to work toward biblical agreement (Philippians 4:1: "be of one mind in the Lord").

All of this is not merely academic; every aspect of it is bursting with practical significance. There are numerous applications of the biblical principles of Church authority that are vital for the well being of the Church as she endeavors to serve her Lord in the everyday ongoing affairs of life. For instance, consider the following:

1. If Christ expects the members of His Church to respect the authority that He has given to His undershepherds, as I have indicated, they must be *taught* to do so. The widespread lack of respect for such authority in the Church today clearly indicates that there is a mammoth educational task in this regard that must be undertaken by every minister. The fact, then, is that the possession of authority from Christ implies the responsibility to *teach* about authority (cf. Titus 2:15).

2. If Christ expects the members of His flock to obey His undershepherds, then they must *exercise* that authority. They may not preach and act "as the Pharisees," but they must speak as Christ: "with authority." That is to say, the possession of authority requires the need for careful, but courageous, full and firm use of that authority.

3. If Christ has given undershepherds to lead His flock and He expects them to follow this leadership, then ministers of the gospel must *exert true shepherdly leadership*. That is to say, leadership must be personal and involved; such need for leadership implies the necessity for personal holiness of example and walk in the Christian life. The authoritative uniform must be filled by one whose life is submitted to that authority.

4. If shepherds wish to exercise biblical leadership with authority, they themselves *must know and teach the Scriptures faithfully in depth*. That is to say, both leadership and authority imply the need for shepherds with biblical knowledge and wisdom.

5. If they care about exercising powerful leadership, shepherds must be willing to *support every plan, every program and every administrative act by scriptural principles.* That is to say, they will ever study, question, examine and reexamine everything that they say or do as leaders in the light of the Word of God — they will never be satisfied with custom and tradition alone.

6. Whenever they cannot support their actions with certain assurance of biblical backing or whenever they are unsure about the teachings of the Scriptures concerning a given point of faith or life, shepherds may not require compliance from members of the flock to what can be only a tentative (and possibly erroneous) position. That is to say, authority must be used within the limits and according to the teaching of the Word of God, and its use, therefore, implies *the need for great discernment and careful judgment by undershepherds.*

Because shepherdly authority and leadership are ministerial, and these elements are sheep-oriented, they exist for the benefit of the flock, and for the good of each member of the flock. They are means for enabling all to grow by grace. That is to say, authority and leadership *must be exercised in love, with care, and with concern* both for the welfare of the flock and of each sheep in it.

8. Since all authority is Christ's authority, it *must be used in His Name and for His glory.* That is to say, authority implies concern for the honor of Christ in every instance of its use.

These eight implications, and their practical effects, are not exhaustive but merely suggestive of some of the more important implications of the concept of shepherdly leadership.

Obedience in Secondary Situations

Questions arise about the secondary aspects of leadership however. Since shepherdly leaders are to be "obeyed" (Hebrews 13:17) and "followed" or "imitated" (Hebrews 13:7), it seems clear that in those matters not specifically ordered by the Scriptures, about which the leaders are obligated to make decisions, the members must submit to their leadership *unless what is enjoined plainly violates biblical requirements.* Otherwise the leadership exercised would be merely declarative and not managerial. For instance, the Scriptures teach that the Church is to meet on the first day of the week for worship; the leaders, therefore, have no authority to decide to hold the regular weekly services on Tuesdays instead. But the Scriptures do not set a specific hour for worship, nor do they require any stated number of such convocations on the first day. Because it is incumbent upon the leadership to see to it that the saints assemble themselves *together* and that in doing so order is maintained and confusion is eliminated (cf. I Corinthians 14:33,40), they must determine how many meetings there will be and when these meetings will be held. The members of the flock should submit to these decisions and order their own affairs to conform to those decisions. Yet, in making such decisions, biblical mandates concerning prudence, concern for the members of the flock, etc., should lead them to consider matters of practicality (e.g., if most of the members are dairy farmers, it would be disruptive to hold services at the milking hour). Members may disagree with the wisdom of the leaders' judgments in such matters and may respectfully request (or even urge) changes, but they have no right to refuse to comply unless they can show clearly that compliance would require them to disobey God. In matters of disagreement about such issues, the elders in the church (like the husband in the home) must have the last word.

But leaders within the Church of Christ do not merely "manage" or "rule." In addition, part of their *leadership* function is to teach, to train, to plan, to organize and to encourage others. And a large share of their work consists of developing the flock itself into a smoothly functioning organism in which each member contributes fully to the operation of the whole (Ephesians 4:15,16). We must turn therefore to the study of a fundamental principle of leadership found in that significant passage. But first, let me issue an important warning.

Management by Divine Direction

While I cannot spend a large amount of space here discussing the problem, I do wish to warn pastors not to adopt business models for the government of the Church of Jesus Christ. There has been too much easy adaptation of pagan principles and practices by evangelical churches in recent times; and the area of leadership and administration has not escaped this baneful trend. One typical sort of problem is the wholesale takeover of Bible-believing congregations by the Management By Objective movement. Some, in the most naively uncritical manner, have accepted it as the greatest boon to the church since the conversion of the apostle Paul. I cannot agree.

The Church of the Lord Jesus Christ is not merely a human organization; it was not created by men, nor was it intended to serve purely human needs. Therefore, many of its *objectives* (for example) will not be realized in time but only in eternity. Moreover, objectives of both sorts (eternal, temporal) are not always subject to quantifiable measurement.

How, for instance, can a pastor judge the amount of sanctification of the believer in the pew at any point? Indeed, he has been forbidden to do so. The Scriptures assure him that only God looks on the heart. He has been told that human judgments will prove false: many of the first shall be last, and the last first. Yet, one of the key objectives of the Church is to help the believer to grow by the grace of God ministered to him. The emphasis upon measurable ends (goals and objectives) may encourage the church to develop a pragmatic mentality and may obscure the need for adopting only those goals and using only those means that snugly fit into the biblical principles and presuppositions. Not all ends are acceptable to God, nor is every means that may be used to attain those ends.

Instead of heralding the advent of usable business practices as the salvation of the church, it is time to emphasize the glorious fact that the Church has at its head a divine King who not only rules and guides her by His Spirit through His Word, but that He does this by the means that He has ordained. He leads the Church toward the goals and objectives which He Himself has articulated. The Church is not free to set its own goals and objectives, or to adopt its own means. All legitimate goal-setting and means-using that goes beyond the foundational revealed goals and means, at every point must grow out of and depend upon those which are scripturally revealed. Such goals and means, therefore, always will be of a secondary, derived and short term nature. Any help that may be obtained from Management By Objective, PERT or other business and management schemes must be subjected to strenuous evaluation in the full light of all of the foundational biblical principles. Otherwise (and this is what has happened) the Bible will be by-passed or accommodated to fit the secular scheme.

The pastor must remember that unlike the businessman, he has divine direction available. His situation truly is unique. In this he should rejoice. The organization in which he functions was "built" by the Lord Jesus and was given its commission by Him. Means which may at times seem not too effective (preaching, for instance) may not be abandoned in favor of what may be hoped to be more effective ones. The King of the church has given orders: "preach the Word ... in season and *out of season.*" The church has no option about the matter. Her only problem is to improve that preaching; she may not question whether the means is to be continued or not on the basis of whether it is looked upon as foolish. The Lord, through Paul, has already pointed out that in the eyes of unconverted men the preaching of the Word is foolishness. On strictly business principles, preaching probably should be abandoned.

The pastor must recognize that the Scriptures are the basic Management

Guide for the church. Any ways or means, and goals or objectives that do not accord with that Guide must be abandoned or modified so that they do. The practice of running off after the latest ideas cooked up in the American Management Association think tanks must give way to more mature evaluation. The greatest danger is for preachers who are discouraged over the growth of their congregations, to walk wide-eyed into the conferences held by well-meaning Christian businessmen, and buy the tempting wares that they find displayed on every shelf. These businessmen usually have little regard for the biblical principles of church government, little knowledge of the theology that undergirds the objectives of the church and little ability (or concern) to do the painstaking exegesis that is necessary to acquire criteria by which to evaluate the world's products that they are wholesaling. Pastor you must beware. You have a Standard of faith and practice, and you should not be surprised to find that this Standard differs radically from the latest pronouncements of the A.M.A. Why should not the church run smoothly if she seriously follows the directions of her Head and King? Should not the A.M.A. take a leaf from the church now and then?

Consider some facts. For one thing, the analogy of the church and a business is not exact. Indeed, while the church is likened to many other organizations in the Scriptures (a flock of sheep, a family, a kingdom), it is not compared to a business organization.[5] Naturally there are similarities, but it is my contention that the differences (which are many) have not been taken seriously. For instance, one would expect to find differences of the sort that exist between a business and a political organization, since the church is God's *kingdom*. In politics not everything is done with profit as the sole objective; there are other considerations as well (international relations, etc.). The differences between a business and a *family* (which like a political government does have a business side) also must be taken into account. For one thing, elements of parental and brotherly love will strongly influence decisions made by the family; an influence that surely would never enter the minds of the hard-headed captains of industry, let alone direct their planning conferences. So you can see even from these brief considerations that the uncritical adoption of the business model for applications to the management of the church is unsound and dangerous.

Uncritical Adoption of Business Practices

I say *uncritical* because it is in that aspect of the problem that the danger

---

[5] *Aspects* of business life are appealed to (cf. Matthew 13:45), but while Christians are called sheep, brothers, etc., they are not called *businessmen*.

lies. A Christian is uncritical in adopting an objective, a goal or practice (1) when he has not searched the Scriptures first to see if they speak directly to the matter under consideration, (2) when he fails to test it by the Scriptures from every angle, (3) when he unwittingly brings the branch, trunk, roots and dirt along with the leaf, and (4) when, having assured himself that there is adequate reason for the adoption of a principle or practice, he fails to shape it to fit the Bible but instead allows it to bend the Bible out of shape to make room for it. It is my conviction that this has been done far too often (and far too readily) not only in the area of counseling (about which I have been speaking for some time)[6] but in other crucial areas of church life as well. One of these areas is management and administration. Insofar as the church allows itself to be managed by the world's principles, she can expect to run into problems with God. *He* is running the church and He will have it run *His way!*

Pastors must consider it of prime importance, therefore, not to allow the church to be run strictly according to business principles. Businessmen in the congregation may clamor for more efficiency, etc. (and their pleas must be heeded if the church has become inefficient), but they must not (as a result) be allowed to reshape the church by the principles of business and management. The church must be shaped by her sovereign Lord!

EXERCISE

For the Student and the Pastor

Obtain some business and management materials. Make a casual survey of these materials and list:

1. Practices that are in conflict with the Scriptures.

---

[6]On this subject, see especially my recent book *Your Place in the Counseling Revolution* (Presbyterian & Reformed Pub. Co., Nutley, N. J.:1975), chapters 2 and 3.

2. Practices that, carefully adapted in a critical manner, could serve the church.

CHAPTER THREE
LEADERSHIP MEANS EQUIPPING OTHERS

Consider the fundamental principle of biblical leadership that is found in Ephesians 4:11,12:

> And he gave some as apostles, and some as prophets, and some as evangelists, and some as pastors and teachers, for the equipping of the saints for the work of service, to the building up of the body of Christ.

Probably there is no more important criterion by which to measure the administration in the modern church than that which is found in this verse. Let us therefore, take time to open up the verse, together with a few of its implications. This vital passage indicates that the leaders of the church are "given" by the risen, triumphant Christ to His Church. Unfortunately, this is a gift that too often has been set on the shelf and forgotten, failing to recognize its true purpose and importance. This gift does not have an ornamental but rather a practical purpose. The pastor-teacher (in the original these two terms are united in such a way that it is clear that they are used to designate one and the same person[1]) was given for the expressed purpose of equipping the saints[2] for *their* work of ministry. This equipping, in turn, has as its goal enabling the entire body to build itself up in love (v.16). The fundamental principle to note is that biblical leadership has in view the *challenging and equipping of the whole flock for ministry* (cf. especially Hebrews 13:20,21 where the "Great Shepherd of the sheep" is called upon to *"equip you in every good thing to do His will"[3]).*

---

[1]This fact I have indicated by the hyphen: the "shepherd-teacher"; or "pastor-teacher."

[2]I.e., the whole body; all of the sheep in the flock. The word *Saints* means: "those who have been set apart" by God from sin to righteousness. It is used in the New Testament to designate living persons (all true Christians).

[3]The word equip is *Katartizo,* the same word that is used in Ephesians 4:12 and, incidentally, in II Timothy 3:17 (in a slightly different form).

The very important corollary to that principle is that neither the pastor, nor the elders should attempt to do any of the work for which God holds the whole body responsible. As members of that body, of course, the pastors and the elders must become involved. But, as *officers,* it is not their duty to step in and do for him what Christ has called any member to do himself. Whenever he does so, the shepherd preempts the blessings that belong to the member, deprives the whole body of the benefits that are intended for it, and fails to challenge and train him for his ministry. Instead, in following the principle set forth in Ephesians 4:11,12 he must make every effort to encourage and enable the delinquent member to assume his proper role for Christ.

Let us take a typical example of an area in which this principle speaks to a problem commonly seen in evangelical churches — the evangelistic outreach of the local congregation. Let us assume, as is so often the case, that the members of the congregation do little or no evangelism. They expect the evangelistic work of the church to be planned and executed by the pastor himself. ("After all, what else does he have to do between Sundays?" and "What do you think we pay him for?") In such instances, what does a new pastor (or a pastor who has become newly aware of his biblical responsibilities in regard to this matter) do?

Well, let us answer first by describing what so many pastors do. Frequently, because he is concerned about the unsaved members of the community around him, after failing to get an immediate favorable response to an appeal for help from the flock, the pastor launches out into a personal evangelism program *on his own.* That is to say, he steps squarely into the center of the trap that has been spread before him. I am not condemning either his zeal or his concern; both are commendable. But zeal unbridled by the Scriptures is like a runaway stallion!

What has he done? Let us analyze both the decision itself and its effects in some detail, since together, they constitute a formidable problem that illustrates the cause of much of the weakness found in the contemporary church. Not infrequently does this weakness stem from the fundamental error in the conduct of biblical leadership that may be seen in this decision. It is the error of failing to understand and/or to follow the basic principle of shepherdly leadership enjoined in Ephesians 4:11,12.

Again, let me ask, what has he done? The answer is this: the pastor has determined, contrary to his call and ordination (which was primarily to shepherd and teach his flock) to devote to the work of evangelism a significant proportion of the time that he ought to spend as pastor-teacher.

Now, please do not misunderstand. I do not think that he should fail to do evangelism both as an individual Christian, *and as a pastor-teacher.*[4] While he should "do the work of an evangelist" (II Timothy 4:5), both as a Christian (i.e., as a member of God's flock) and as an example to the flock (cf. I Timothy 4:12, but especially Titus 2:7, where "in all things" Titus is exhorted to "be an example of good works," one of which is the work of evangelism),[5] and while he might be involved in as much (or even more) evangelism as any other member of the body, that does not mean that he should try to do any of the work of evangelism *that belongs to each member of the flock.* He must remember that it is true not only biologically, but also in evangelism, that it is sheep — not shepherds — who must produce other sheep.[6]

When a pastor on his own tries to do the work of an entire congregation,

1. He fails because he does not have the blessing of Christ upon this program; he has substituted (well-meaningly, perhaps, but none-the-less highhandedly *substituted)* a human plan for the divine one.[7]

2. He fails because he does not have the many opportunities and contacts that *only* the members of his congregation have.

3. He fails because he spreads himself too thin, trying to do too much as one person. It is nothing less than pride for any one individual to think that he is capable of doing what God has said is the work of an entire congregation.

4. He fails also as a pastor-teacher. In spreading himself so thinly over the works of evangelism as well as that of shepherding and of teaching, he does none of these things well. His sermons suffer, his members are not cared for and even the fruit of the evangelism usually is minimal.

5. He fails — and this is the most significant failure of all — because, wittingly or unwittingly, he has disobeyed and thereby dishonored the Chief Shepherd by whom he had been "given" to the Church in order to shepherd and teach so that the sheep might discover, develop and deploy

---

[4]If he spends time *teaching* evangelism, both formally and by example, that is a needed and legitimate use of time. One of the shepherdly tasks to which he is called is to equip the saints to evangelize.

[5]Cf. also I Peter 5:3 where those who oversee as shepherds are told to lead not by "lording it over" the flock, but by "proving to be examples to the flock." In evangelism, as in all other good works, the shepherd of the sheep should "lead them out" and "go before them." Sheep must be led, not driven.

[6]That is not to say, of course, that he should not evangelize in counseling or even in his pastoral preaching. In the pastoral messages that he preaches, he should relate every passage to the great redemptive theme that is the fundamental and evangelistic message of the Bible. But, while in every sermon he makes the gospel known, that does not mean that he preaches nothing but the gospel. He must remember Hebrews 6:1ff.

[7]Not that God may not use this failure providentially to bring about His own purposes, which *may* include the birth of many lambs into the fold (cf. Philippians 1:15-18).

their own gifts. Thus he fails to equip each member for his own "work of ministry (including the ministry of evangelism, which, in part, belongs to every believer).[8]

Let us spend a few minutes more considering this all-too-frequent problem that is illustrative of the general failure of shepherds to devote themselves to the work to which they have been called.[9]

The Chief Shepherd knows best; His orders must be obeyed and His plan must be followed. It is not the part of undershepherds to take it upon themselves to determine other goals and methods. To do so is rebellion against the Chief Shepherd who wishes not only the shepherds but also the sheep to be "equipped" to *"do His will."* How can sheep be expected to follow God's revealed will when the shepherds do not do so? Their bad example (however well-meant) is culpable; it is nothing short of sin. No wonder the Church of Christ suffers so!

But sin is also always foolish. Consider, therefore, how utterly foolish alternate plans appear when they are compared and contrasted with the biblical one. Perhaps the best way to develop this point is to take a hard look at the way in which the Holy Spirit shepherded the evangelistic enterprise in the early Church. Surely, by way of contrast, it is instructive to compare the rapid growth of the New Testament Church (cf. Colossians 1:6: "in all the world," 1:23: "the gospel"..."which was proclaimed in all creation under heaven," Acts 12:24; 19:10,20) with the disturbingly slow progress and meagre impact made in so many communities in modern times. While the contrast in the evangelistic approaches used is vivid, of course this difference in itself does not entirely account for the difference in results. Nevertheless, in some large measure, the modern failure may be traced to this difference, since in those instances today where the biblical approach has been followed, similar results frequently have been

---

[8]Cf. Jay Adams *Shepherding God's Flock*, Vol. II of this series.

[9]Illustratively, I say, because the problem extends into many areas. For instance, in the work of shepherdly administration many pastors fail to call upon elders and deacons (not to speak of other members of the flock) to help them as they should, either preferring to do it themselves ("The only way to get a job done is to do it yourself.") or giving up when an immediate response is not forthcoming after an appeal for help. (The failure in this case actually may be due to dependence upon the scripturally dubious practice of volunteerism; this will be discussed *infra*). The pastor is *not* directed merely to challenge members to assume their ministries, but rather is required to teach (i.e., to show them biblically both their responsibility to minister, and how to go about discharging this responsibility) and to shepherd the flock (i.e., to lead and guide them by precept and example—an example that provides the living integration of truth in experience). The Chief Shepherd, through His undershepherds, thus "equips" them for "every good work." Apart from this pastor-teaching work, sheep will find it difficult to respond to the challenge (even when put to them properly)

obtained.[10] When you add to this failure the fact that many pastors have abandoned other biblical patterns or substituted their own programs for them (e.g., failure to adopt patterns of administrative delegation, the failure to exercise church discipline, etc.) you can begin to understand the basic reason for the weakness of the modern church.

To continue to etch out the biblical picture in stark contrast to modern substitutes, let me pursue the matter of evangelism a bit more fully.

The early Church moved out of its first stage (preach the gospel in Jerusalem) into the second (and in all Judea and Samaria) not as an evangelistic effort headed by the apostles.[11] Indeed, when in God's providence the persecution under Saul drove the church out of its bottled up condition in Jerusalem, Luke specifically records the fact that the apostles were not personally involved in that evangelistic thrust ("and they were all scattered throughout the regions of Judea and Samaria, *except the apostles,*" Acts 8:2b). So those who went into those regions were not the leaders but everyday, man-in-the-pew Christians of the Church of Jerusalem.

Note next what they did: "Those who were scattered abroad went about announcing the message of good news" (Acts 8:4, literal translation). They presented the gospel to everyone they met. They did not invite people to church meetings, they did not take surveys in the community; they evangelized (i.e., they announced the good news about Christ). To present the gospel is to announce the good news about what has been *done* by Christ. The good news is not a command or exhortation to do something to save one's self (it is proper to exhort someone to repent and believe the good news, but that is not the good news itself). What, then, is the good news? Paul tells us in I Corinthians 15:1,4. Notice, as you read these verses how the news itself contains two elements, both of which were prophesied in the Old Testament ("according to the Scriptures"):

> Now I make known to you brethren, the gospel (good news) which I preached to you...that Christ died for our sins according to the Scriptures, and that He was buried, and that He was raised on the third day according to the Scriptures.

---

[10]Not invariably. It is, of course, God's task to produce the results (I Corinthians 3:6,7). There are times when faithful work does not produce fruit (cf. Isaiah 6:9-13). Yet, it is always the responsibility of the Church, by His grace, to do as He has commanded. Results of some sort then may be expected, for His Word never returns "void." At times the results may be persecution rather than belief.

[11]The Holy Spirit outlined His three-stage evangelistic program in Acts 1:8b. In a vital sense the Book of Acts is based upon this program and amounts to an unfolding of the verse.

Nothing more, nothing less is the gospel. A careful study of every recorded proclamation of the good news in the Book of Acts, whether in personal evangelism or in a public sermon, shows without exception that those two points were always stressed. The same good news must be proclaimed today.

Now, back to the main point concerning organization: in the early church, everyone evangelized everywhere.[12] When this again occurs in the modern church, there will be a return of New Testament power.

Look at the two organizational patterns in contrast.

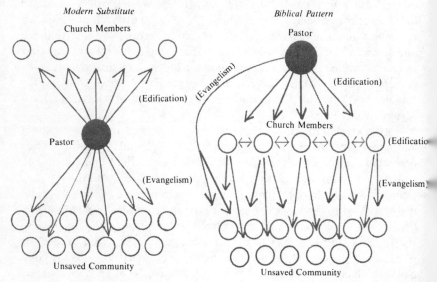

According to this faulty, foolish unbiblical model, the congregation hires a minister to do its work of evangelism. This arrangement is impossible. It is a full time task to shepherd and teach (edification). One man cannot do that and, in addition, hope to reach the multitudes around him as well. Truly, on this plan, the pastor is in the middle. Nor is the flock taught to engage in edification with the pastor.

According to the biblical model, the pastor and teacher is just that. He instructs, equips, and inspires the congregation to assume its own evangelistic and edificational ministry (note arrows between members). He also evangelizes as a Christian and as the leading example for the members of the local church.

---

[12]The description of a full program entitled *Everyone Evangelizing Everywhere,* based upon this passage, will be found in Appendix A.

EXERCISE

For the Student

1. List the ways and means that you have been equipped by your congregation for ministry.

2. List the ways and means that you have been equipped to evangelize.

For the Pastor
   1. How does your church actively equip saints for ministry?

2. What are some ways in which you could improve upon your present program for doing so?

CHAPTER FOUR
DELEGATION AND SHARING

It is important at this point to look closely at two vital guiding principles of shepherdly leadership and oversight: the scriptural principles of delegation and sharing.

Delegation, in the Scriptures, is inherent in the concepts of scriptural leadership and management. For instance, one who "manages his own household well" may do so to a great extent through the encouragement that he gives to a resourceful Christian wife (like the one mentioned in Proverbs 31 who herself "looks well to the ways of her household," v. 27). To her he may entrust many of those matters for which God will hold *him* responsible as the head of his home. If, indeed, she is a woman who is husband oriented and will "do him good and not harm all the days of her life" (31:12), he may safely put much authority into her hands. When the "heart of her husband trusts in her" in this way, he is able to rely upon her efforts as a valuable (Proverbs says priceless) asset in carrying out the functions of the home for which God will hold him responsible. Such managerial activity in the church likewise involves delegation of much of the work.

With the delegation of duties, there is, however, the retention of responsibility and accountability. What the husband delegates to his wife, God still holds *him* responsible for. That means that he cannot pass the buck of responsibility to his wife. He must consider himself responsible to God for what she does and for what she does not do. Of course, from her perspective, she is responsible to her husband under God. That means that he must (1) be sure that she is *capable* of doing what he delegates to her before he does so, (2) be certain that she is *willing* to accept the responsibility, (3) continually *keep in touch* with the work that she is doing so that he knows at all times what is happening and (4) *be ready and able to step in* when she needs help, or to do trouble-shooting should the occasion arise.

What is true concerning the possibility of the delegation of duties to others in the home, also holds true in the church. It is interesting to notice how Paul parallels home management with church management in I Timothy 3:4,5. It is not inappropriate, therefore, to ask when considering a man for the position of pastor-teacher, whether (in the home) he tries to do everything himself. How, for instance, does he understand and apply the principles of headship and submission? Does he exercise headship in terms of the principle of delegation demonstrated in Proverbs 31? A man who refuses to use all of the resources that God has provided by giving him a capable wife, and who fails to value her role in the marriage as his helper by happily soliciting her help whenever possible, will not make a good elder. He will find that he has similar problems in delegating work and receiving help from others in the congregation. It is the pastor's duty to put people to work at the tasks that God intended them to do. He must give evidence of willingness and ability to fulfill this duty before he is eligible for ordination as a ruler in Christ's Church. I shall return to the matter of delegation at a later point.

Sharing Work

Paul, in I Timothy 5:17 distinguishes between elders who only "preside" or "manage" and elders who also labor at preaching and teaching. The latter are elders to whom has been committed the role of pastor-teacher. The important fact to note is that there are some elders, who, while they do not share in the work of preaching and teaching do act jointly with the pastor-teacher to carry out the work of administration. This concept of *sharing* the managerial work of the local congregation among the elders is of vital importance. God has provided for a plurality of church governors in the local congregation to carry the burden of responsibility and of effort *with* the pastor-teacher. Yet too often church government by elders is minimized in the modern church (1) by pastors who like to make the decisions themselves (many of whom think "if you want something done right, do it yourself"), and (2) by elders and pastors who look on the ruling elder as someone who attends meetings, debates and votes, but does not actually get involved in the performance of administrative tasks.

Such minimizing of management by elders in large measure accounts for the administrative overload of the minister. Failure to share this administrative load with all of those who preside over a congregation amounts to robbing the elders of the blessings of their call and turns their work into a purely academic task. This failure, moreover, gives them great opportunity to become hypercritical, since they do not have to face the realities of church management themselves. Again, when the pastor endeavors to carry burdens that are too heavy for one man to bear alone, the elders soon will find more than enough to criticize. Much unnecessary dissension arises from this failure to share administration with elders at the level where the rubber meets the road.

From the early days of the organized church of God in the Old Testament, elders helped to bear the load. When Moses attempted to carry the work of ruling his people alone, he soon found that it became too great for him (Exodus 18:18). So, following Jethro's suggestion, he secured others to judge and to become "heads over the people" (Exodus 18:25[1]) together with him. He still handled the most difficult problems personally, while the others judged those cases that were more-or-less routine (v. 26). Together, they *shared* the work. Thus by this expedient Moses was able to discharge his responsibilities before God.

Moses' willingness to adopt the suggestion of his father-in-law demonstrates that there is a certain amount of proper flexibility about how one may discharge a responsibility. This flexibility, in particular, involves the right to share and to delegate his duties. Yet whenever one shares or delegates, the responsibility always finally rests upon the one whose task it was originally.

Later, we read that God appointed seventy men from among the elders of the people and gave them each a part of the Spirit Who was upon Moses. These men, God said, "shall bear the burden of the people *with you*, so that you shall not bear it *alone*" (Numbers 11:17). The principle of sharing one's task seems prominent in both of these passages.

The continuity of this eldership runs unbroken through the Old Testament (whether there were periods in which prophets, judges or kings also might rule) and right into the book of Acts, where without so much as a word of explanation, of distinction or whatever, Luke moves in one breath from mention of the Jewish eldership to mention of the eldership of the New Testament Church. The transition is so smooth, so natural, so clear that there can be no reasonable doubt that Luke saw the Church's eldership as constituting nothing less than a direct succession from the Old Testament order. Continuity is everywhere apparent: the New Testament assumes much knowledge about church government; there is a decided lack of explicit details, there is a free wheeling use of titles without explanation, etc. One thing is clear, from beginning to end, congregations are described as having a plurality of elders all of whom share in the management of the church.

---

[1]Cf. also Deuteronomy 1:9-15.

Thus, it is vital to understand that delegation and sharing of specific tasks represent two similar, but distinct principles of church management that every pastor must recognize and employ. No minister of the gospel can bear up under the burdens of the governing ministry alone. The picture of a pastor-teacher sharing congregational management with ruling elders, and the delegation of ministry to others within the congregation, gives a much more accurate sketch of biblical church administration than the one commonly seen in the modern church.

Deacons

Yet, not all has been said to complete the biblical picture. Acts 6 describes the origin of the New Testament diaconate, a body of men whose specific calling is to help elders and pastor-teachers by relieving them of numerous administrative details that otherwise might pull them away from the work to which God has called them. When they observed that it was improper for them to serve tables, the apostles were not speaking in a superior attitude, nor were they looking upon such work as "menial" and therefore not appropriate for men engaged in "spiritual" work. No such haughty dichotomy existed either in their thinking or actions.[2] The diaconate was spawned, because the apostles recognized that they could not do *everything* and that if they were to remain true to their calling, they would have to place so high a priority upon that work that they could not allow themselves to be diverted from it by a necessary, important, spiritual, but decidedly *different sort of activity* that would be time consuming. Consequently, they chose to *delegate* the task of the distribution of funds to men of high quality, whose lives were full of the Holy Spirit. They knew what needed to be done, were concerned to see it done well and therefore provided a vehicle that would assure its satisfactory accomplishment.

What is the diaconate? Is it merely a board designed to collect and distribute funds to the needy and poor? Certainly that task was assigned to the original deacons. But the particular issue that occasioned the selection of those deacons called forth a response from the apostles that shows that their function may be conceived of in wider terms. The basic principle behind the diaconate (a "service" or "ministry" board as the word *deacon* indicates) is to give to the pastor-teacher and to the elders whatever help they need to carry on their calling without diversion or distraction. Unfortunately, again and again congregations fail to use their deacons for

---

[2] Indeed the work of the diaconate is Spiritual (i.e., Spirit-motivated, directed and empowered) work (cf. Acts 6:3,5 in which there is specific mention of the Holy Spirit's presence in connection with the task).

this vital ministry.[3] Yet, again and again pastors, elders and others can be heard complaining that there is no one to carry out the hundred-and-one small (but important) details that make all of the difference in the smooth functioning of Christ's church. Why should they expect persons to respond to such complaints when they have never been given the authority, the training or the responsibility to do so? Moreover, when general appeals for help are broadcast the responses that are forthcoming may not be the most desirable. Volunteerism is a dangerous practice for which biblical warrant probably cannot be found. Surely when it is substituted for work belonging to deacons it is wrong. Persons who are not fitted for duties may respond so that in the end one might conclude that it would have been better not to solicit help after all. However, in analyzing the situation, it usually turns out that the sense that help was needed was correct; what was wrong was the method by which the help was requested. When a congregation has a vital board of deacons, selected according to the biblical criteria found in Acts 6:3 and in I Timothy 3:8-13, *help of the right sort* is always available.

What, then, is the proper role of the deacon? The diaconate is a board of men chosen by the congregation and ordained by God (and the visible Church through the elders), to serve under the elders (they are fully accountable to the elders who, under God, "preside over" or manage *all* of the activities of the local congregation) as helpers whose task is to relieve the pastor and the elders of any and all administrative details that they assign to them. That means that while the elders are spending their time dealing with a difficult matter of church discipline, let us say, they do not have to take out time to organize the next fellowship supper, or to solve some problem with the ushers or with the florist concerning the flowers for the front of the church, or ... (and, here, you can fill in a hundred small time-consuming tasks necessary to the well-being of the flock). The diaconate is a tremendously important catch-all body that no congregation can afford to do without. The deacon's work is *service:* service to God, to the congregation, to the elders and to the pastor-teacher. The pastor-teacher who does not develop a well-functioning diaconate will find that he has lost one of the essential keys that unlock the secret of good church government.

The Delegation of Delegated Work

Of course, the deacons too may learn to delegate. It is possible that in the

---

[3]One reason for not using deacons adequately is the anomaly of the trustee. Trustees are not a biblical office and should never be assigned the duties of the deacon (except possibly aspects *delegated* by them). Trustees are a legal entity designed to represent the church to the state. Trustees should *always* be elected from the elders and deacons.

discharge of their responsibilities they may delegate portions of these to persons within the congregation who have peculiar gifts for ministry. While retaining their own responsibility to the elders and to the pastor, they may solicit particular persons to engage in specific tasks (eg., to usher, to cook, to head up a telephone communications system within the congregation, to type and do secretarial work for the pastor, to provide transportation for the young people, etc.). In one sense, they become the ways and means committee of the congregation.

Within the principle of sharing, a secondary consideration may be appropriate. It involves the utilization of gifts. While *either* the husband or the wife in the home may have the ability and willingness to keep the financial records for the family, it is neither necessary or desirable for *both* of them to do so. They must decide, therefore, who will do what. Everything need not be done in duplicate. So, too, within the eldership and within the diaconate, while every member must have all the qualities necessary for doing all of the work required by those offices, it is not necessary for every man to do every job himself. In Christ's organization of the apostles, for instance, Judas (not all of them) carried the bag. Indeed, since everyone does not have every gift in the same proportion,[4] some may *excel* in one or another aspect of the work of congregational management. While it would be unwise to serve only in those areas in which one excels, it might be important to the whole body for an elder or deacon to *focus* his efforts upon those areas.

Moreover, at different periods in his life a man may utilize his gifts in distinct ways. For example, five years ago, when he was a deacon, a man may have developed and utilized certain capacities and particular skills more fully than he does now that he has become an elder. His *emphasis* now may be upon other matters. Before he became a pastor, a man may have spent a much larger proportion of his time doing evangelism, but now since he has been ordained as a pastor-teacher the *emphasis* of his ministry must change to edification. When Moses shared his work with the judges, we noticed, he reserved the more difficult cases for himself and farmed out the more routine ones. The pastor, as a result of his more specialized training, also may wish to do so in some area. On the other hand, an elder with greater financial ability may be able to carry out some of the aspects of financial budgeting better than the pastor or others.

Sharing of work, then, does not necessarily mean exact conformity or duplication of work by those who share it. Sharing means:

---

[4]Cf. Romans 12:6; 1 Corinthians 12:6.

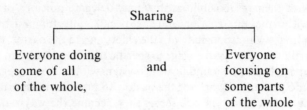

Sharing

Everyone doing
some of all   and
of the whole,

Everyone
focusing on
some parts
of the whole

While certain decisions must be made by all, and certain efforts require the participation of all, various aspects of the work may be apportioned to particular elders or deacons. For example, the details for utilization of the media of communication may be put into the hands of one individual, who also may be peculiarly responsible for publicity since these two areas often converge. He, in turn, may wish to delegate some aspects of the work to others.[5] What he does will be directed by the basic decisions of the whole body, of course, and he will report back to them as he carries out their desires.

Committees

It is tragic when hours of time are consumed by the whole group as everyone attempts to do the work that could be committed to one person. This raises the question of the overuse and misuse of committees. While committees have a valid place, the work of the church has been greatly impeded by too great a dependence upon the committee structure. To lean heavily upon committees rather than upon persons is contrary to the spirit of the New Testament which focuses upon the use of individual gifts for individual ministry to the rest of the body.

Groups, of course, should consult together so that individuals may pool and gather wisdom and thus make better decisions; yet the implementation of those decisions largely must be done by individuals. It is not a wise use of the time of the whole body to decide in a committee meeting how to arrange for transportation to the church picnic when one member of the group is capable of doing this himself. Enough has been accomplished by the whole

---

[5]But one must be sure not to overdelegate; there can be too much of a good thing. Overdelegation breaks down communication and tends to fracture the body. Specialized interests tend to pull a person too far out of the mainstream of the work. Special interests must always contribute to the rest of the body. The eye and the ear must recognize not only their interdependence, but also their purpose in relationship to the whole. Overdelegation has occurred whenever (1) the person first delegating is unfamiliar with the work being done by others to whom his delegatee has delegated it; (2) when someone at, or near, the bottom of a delegation chain is so far removed from the top that he does not recognize the role his work plays in the total picture.

diaconate if the decision to provide transportation has been made, there is an initial input of general ideas, and a trusted individual is appointed to plan and carry out the project.

What is left as a committee's responsibility is really no one's responsibility. That is one reason why it is so easy to proliferate committees; people who do not like to be held accountable know that they may escape that pressure on a committee. Committees tend to shield persons from responsibility. When did you last hear of a committee being reprimanded? It is individuals therefore, who always should be made accountable for specific tasks even when they must enlist the services of others to help them. As a rule of thumb, committees should be used for communicating information, for general discussion and for study; not for detailed work or for taking concrete action. And, then, the committee structure should be used only when the sort of work committed can be done in no other way. To say it the other way around, a committee should be established only whenever the advantages of group activity clearly outweigh those of individual activity.

There are valid reasons for group activity, of course; pooling of information, coordination of activities, communication, and legitimate compromise. Nevertheless, even when so used, committees quickly should break down and divide distinct aspects of their work, assigning these as areas of responsibility to individuals on the committee. Specific tasks in each area for which he may be held accountable should be committed to each individual. It is also wise to keep committees as small as possible. Since the eldership and the diaconate are, in effect, larger committees, I shall present a sample of how one pastor and his elders break up their tasks. To each task area one or more names of an elder or deacon is assigned. This sample I have reproduced as I received it (omitting names): I have made no changes. On the original adjoining each responsibility was a name (depicted on the chart by a line). This makes it clear to the pastor who is responsible for what tasks at all times. He is not likely to send people to wrong sources, or to suggest that persons take on tasks that already have been assigned, thus unwittingly crossing lines of responsibility and delegation when they are set forth diagrammatically. Moreover, if problems arise in an area, simple reference to the chart identifies the person responsible. This plan may not necessarily represent the way that you or that I would or even should apportion the efforts of a different congregation, but because the plan is comprehensive, I think that you will find it suggestive.

Organizational Chart: Bethel Orthodox Presbyterian Church, Oostburg, Wisconsin, 1973

Donald F. Stanton, pastor

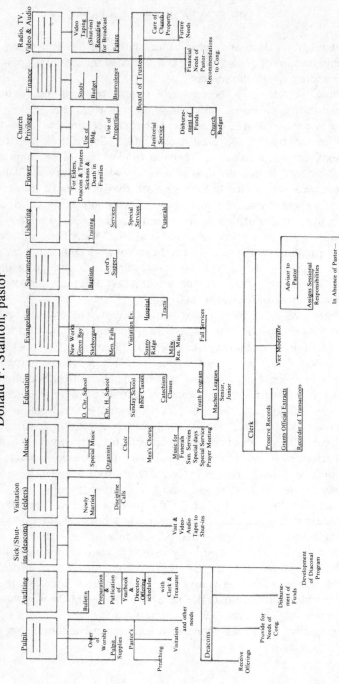

¹Lines indicate names of persons (which I have omitted)

EXERCISE

For the Student and the Pastor

1. Take a careful look at your congregation to see if you can answer the question, "Who is doing what?" about each of the following:

Setting Goals and Priorities _____

Planning the Budget_____

Exercising Control (on paper; in practice) _____

Planning Programs_____

Training Members for Tasks _____

Running the Educational Program _____

Caring for the Buildings and Facilities _____

Working on Publicity_____

Carrying out Evangelism_____

Caring for Guest Speakers _____

Doing Bookkeeping; Keeping Records _____

Regulating Worship _____

Paying Bills _____

Contacting the Florist _____

2. From this survey, suggest ways and means of changing the organizational structure if needed.

For the Pastor

1. Count the number of committees and boards that meet each month to conduct the business of your church:_____

2. Count the number of persons involved in those meetings:_____

3. Count (according to a rough estimate) the number of man hours spent each month just in committee meetings:_____

4. Count the number of hours that *you* spend in committee meetings:_____

If the figures seem too large, they probably are. Try to work out ways of streamlining committee business, principally utilizing the biblical principle of individual gifts (cf. Romans 12:6,8).

CHAPTER FIVE
WORKING WITH THE ELDERSHIP

Probably the first most significant achievement of any minister who newly assumes the pastorate of any congregation is getting to know his elders well and learning how to function smoothly with them. No time can be invested more wisely during the first year of his pastorate (when, as a matter of fact, much else cannot be done anyway) than the time he spends developing and cultivating a close relationship to his elders. This, he should do, both individually and corporately.[1] He must learn to know these men through and through, and he must be willing to expose himself as fully to them as well. A relationship founded upon truth and mutual trust must be built. All of this is essential so that when he tackles the large tasks and faces the crises that inevitably will come, the pastor will not have to do so alone. In many situations, without the full understanding, confidence and backing of his eldership, a minister will be left in a precarious position. His attempts to exert the authority of Christ will be undercut, his efforts to exercise church discipline for the benefit of an erring and contumacious member may be foiled, and his ability to move quickly and smoothly in emergencies will be seriously impaired.

It is important for the new minister not to discount his elders too quickly. It is my observation that this is a fault of many pastors. When one notes how zealously and patiently Paul labored with Timothy over his timidity, it shows (1) that all was not sweetness and light among the elders of the New Testament Church (it is quite wrong to idealize the situation[2]), and (2) that it is wrong to despair of a man with potential, even when he has some glaring faults. Encouragement, giving him the right kind of task (one in which he is very likely to succeed), or a variety of other such efforts could make a great difference in the release and development of that potential.

---

[1] It is best to start properly upon assuming the pastorate; but at least you can begin correcting matters now if you did not previously.

[2] The unrealistic way in which some apply the biblical criteria for elders and deacons not only discourages men with potential, but it seems quite foreign to the New Testament approach.

The pastor should attempt to discover (1) whether there is potential (often gifts can be tested only by trying them out) and (2) whether there is a special reason for the elder's weakness (e.g., the former pastor did everything himself, was afraid of elders growing in power, they received no help or instruction, etc).

In general, the pastor should expect much from his elders and should let them know so. He should assume that they are (or with proper teaching and encouragement will become) willing and able to accomplish great things. What he expects, he will communicate. What he communicates, he will get. If he gives them the impression that they are hopelessly inadequate, more than likely they will turn out to be just that; and he will be sure his judgment was correct! But also he should be clear about his own willingness to help them to become all that God wants them to be. It is no wonder that so little is done by many elders; when you hear how their ministers speak about them, you understand.

Frequently, elders enter upon their work with great enthusiasm and genuine dedication, only to have both cooled in short order by the fact that they are called upon to do nothing but attend meetings and never become involved in the actual work of ministering to their flock. Moreover, even if they are encouraged to take part in such ministry, they are given virtually no instruction about how to do so. If they are instructed at all, usually it will be in doctrine, possibly also in church government, but rarely ever in the principles and skills of personal ministry to human beings. Rather than excoriating them for failure to enter into such work, instead the pastor might inquire about previous expectations and past training. If he finds that these were inadequate, he would be better advised to set up an elders' training program (either formally or informally).[3] All of the exhortation in the world will not suffice when someone does not know *how* to follow it. Consequently, the pastor would do well to encourage his elders to sit in on counseling sessions *with him,* to learn how to conduct home Bible Studies *with him,* to make visits *with him,* etc. The training that most elders lack is discipleship, or on-the-job training. They need to be taught by example.

At first they must be given the opportunity working with the pastor to observe and to participate in such activities under supervision. Next, they may be encouraged to minister for a while on their own. After a time, they

---

[3]An excellent manual by George Scipione, designed to train elders (or potential elders) has been published. There is nothing else like it in print. This manual takes elders through all of the biblical passages pertaining to their qualifications and work in a personal and thoroughly practical way. The book is broken into a series of lessons, each culminating in homework assignments. By all means get a copy if you have not seen it. The handbook, entitled *Timothy Titus, and You,* is available from the Pilgrim Publishing Company, Phillipsburg, N. J.

should gather others from the congregation who show promise, as their disciples, to train them in the same way that they have been trained. Some of these men eventually may develop into deacons or elders.

It is important, I have said, for a pastor to get to know his elders. That takes time but it also takes willingness on the part of the pastor to be warm, friendly, open and truthful to them. Inviting them over to his home, holding elders' retreats for planning, prayer and fellowship in spring and/or fall, and a variety of other elders' activities will be necessary to achieve closeness. Close relationships do not merely happen; they are built.

It is not enough to get to know your elders in the regular elders' meetings. They must come to know you and you must come to know them in a greater variety of contexts. And they need to come to know one another fully as persons too (rather than merely as "that guy who always votes on the other side of an issue"). If the eldership is to become a smoothly functioning body, exerting a powerful force for good in the congregation, its members will have to be molded together into a cohesive entity by effective pastoral leadership. Good leadership means — among other things — creative planning. Do some right away — with reference to your relationship to your elders (see the exercise for the pastor at the end of the chapter).

The openness and honesty that must develop soon between a pastor and his elders is necessary for good communication (cf. Ephesians 4:25). The pastor can foster this by announcing (in his own words, of course) at the very first elder's meeting:

> Gentlemen, I am a sinner, and I shall fail. At times you will be disappointed in me as well as in other members of the congregation. I will need exhortation and help now and then, as indeed, you will too. Therefore, you can expect me to be honest and straightforward with you. If I have any complaints or any concerns, you will hear them from me: you won't hear them first on the grapevine. And I expect to hear your concerns and your opinions directly too. I shall not allow your honesty or your frankness with me to separate us. Rather, I shall always encourage it as I consider it *essential* to the adequate communication that is needed to bind us together. I will appreciate you all the more for your truthfulness. So come to me; don't go to anyone else, whenever you have a suggestion or complaint.

It is important for a younger pastor not to allow age to separate him from the older men on the eldership. It is precisely those men who often will have the most valuable counsel for him. Yet, his tendency will be to drift toward those of his own age. The tendency must be overcome. If anything, *special* attention should be given to this matter. Ordinarily, these older men are even more easily approachable than some of the younger ones, and will be deeply appreciative of any efforts along these lines that he may make. Their counsel often will provide just the balance that a young impetuous man may need. As a general rule, a new pastor ought to give careful consideration to what they say and only for reasons of greatest weight disregard their counsel. The older men frequently provide a continuity with the past. By talking to them about things that have been from time to time, a pastor can understand better the things that are. Congregational attitudes, sensitivities, etc., that are otherwise inexplicable, become meaningful as he can place them in context.[4]

The elders of the people (as the Bible often describes them when speaking of their representative character) provide another vital link in the congregational communication chain. Through their eyes, and from their perspective the pastor can take more accurate soundings from time to time. Perhaps there is no more important link to preserve and to strengthen. The congregational chain often is as strong as its weakest elder link.

In short, let this brief reminder of the necessity of establishing a firm relationship with the elders be heeded. There is no more vital relationship for the pastor to develop and maintain on the highest level possible.

Elders' business meetings ought not be held too frequently. Too many meetings is ordinarily indicative of a group that likes to talk, but achieves little. Setting a closing hour[5] as well as an opening hour (a good practice for most meetings) keeps long winded discussions to a minimum, and tends to make deliberative meetings (as they should be) more decision/action oriented. The body has met to conduct business; that is what should be done. Other meetings for prayer, general discussion, etc., should be held.[6] An elder's weekly prayer breakfast might be in order. A time for prayer and fellowship before the evening worship service, concurrent with the youth meetings, is another possibility. Typed agendas for business meetings help to keep everyone on track, give an idea of how rapidly work is progressing toward the closing hour, etc. Mail or distribute agendas a week ahead and

---

[4]Cf. *The Christian Counselor's Manual*, pp. 218-221 for an example of this.

[5]And be sure that you stick to it.

[6]Business meetings should be kept to a minimum. Instead, *emphasize* the prayer and fellowship meetings by holding them more frequently. It is possible to get along with regular *monthly* business meetings; other meetings might be held on a *weekly* basis. When times of prayer and fellowship predominate, the character of the business meetings will change too. Also much of the inconsequential small talk will disappear. And a good bit of congregational business will be settled informally by consensus outside of the business meeting (as it should be).

urge members to jot down questions and observations on these, and to gather data about the matters to be discussed beforehand.[7] Too much business time is wasted on informing, asking last minute questions, and failure to do prior research. All such matters should be attended to as fully as possible before the meeting itself.

EXERCISE

For the Student

Report on the following:

1. Interview several elders to determine what they know about their office, what they do as elders and what their attitudes about their work may be.

---

[7]But be sure to have extra copies on hand for the meeting. You can count on some members forgetting theirs.

2. Ask them what sort of training for the eldership they have had (if any).

3. Ask the elders what lacks they most keenly recognize and what they think may be done about them.

For the Pastor

Design a yearly program for getting to know your elders better. Be sure to schedule each element.

CHAPTER SIX
WORKING WITH ANOTHER PASTOR

Closely related to the task of working with the eldership, but significantly different, is the possibility of working jointly with associates, and/or assistants in the pastoral-teaching ministry. Some of the principles of sharing mentioned previously should be kept in mind as you read this chapter.

It should go without saying that the "senior" minister must take the lead in establishing and nurturing this relationship, although the responsibilities are, by no means, solely his. For instance, it is usually customary for assistants and associates to give a new "senior" pastor the opportunity to choose his own staff.[1] Yet the new man may be wise to encourage the continuation of the services of previously called associates, at least for a time, for purposes of continuity.

Many observations might be made about such a joint ministry, but let me emphasize only two or three. For one thing, it is a mistake to divide the pastoral labors of the congregation too rigidly. While some division is inevitable, and desirable, a complete dichotomy of labor is unhealthy. Though one principally may preach and another principally may do counseling (for example) it is unwise to make an explicit distinction of this sort. Usually, such sharp distinctions are set forth in titles, such as minister of counseling, minister of youth, etc. Every man who counsels effectively also will want to preach. If he does not, question his ability to counsel, or his real concern for people. He will want to have opportunity to warn against the destructive courses of sin that he sees day after day in the counseling room. If he does not have a preventive ministry as well as a remedial one, on the one hand, he may tend to become unbalanced and warped in his outlook, and, on the other hand, the congregation will suffer from not receiving the benefits of his pulpit ministry. The man who

---

[1]But this implies that associates work for a senior pastor. There is no biblical warrant for this. Both serve God, working side-by-side with elders to shepherd God's flock. The concept of a "senior" pastor, except as he may *by agreement* take the overall leadership, is not biblical.

preaches exclusively, and does no counseling, may tend to become abstract and pedantic. He must continually apply the principles of the Scriptures to real life problems, if his examples and his applications in the pulpit are to ring true. Both men, while *emphasizing* one phase of the work or another, according to the greater or lesser endowment of gifts that they possess, nevertheless must possess *all* of the gifts for all of the work of the ministry or they should not have been ordained in the first place. It is not as if the qualifications in the Pastoral Epistles could be *divided* between them; each man must qualify with reference to the whole. Each man must *balance* his ministry according to Colossians 1:28 (counseling and teaching) and Ephesians 4:11 (pastor and teacher).

This principle of division of emphasis, not of labor, cuts other ways. Whenever a minister devotes his energies largely to youth work, for instance, he must have complete freedom to work also with any other member of the congregation. He must have the opportunity whenever necessary, to call in parents and together with the young people, counsel all of them *as a family*. Otherwise, his ministry *to youth* will be truncated. While mentioning this point, let me observe that it often is desirable for *both* ministers to counsel jointly as a team under such circumstances, especially whenever there has been counseling previously by one or the other (with one segment of the family) that may have a bearing upon the present problem.

In general, let it be said that where there is more than one minister, care must be taken to see that members of the congregation are not allowed to divide them from one another. They must determine to stand back to back. Close, ongoing communication, including a regular exchange of significant information (at least two weekly information exchange conferences seem desirable), is absolutely essential. Ideas, plans, programs, approaches, solutions to problems, must be hammered out and coordinated. A house divided against itself cannot stand. There is no easier way to divide the household of faith than to provide for a congregation two or more leaders who gather factions about themselves.[2] Frank, frequent, prayerful discussion of this matter, leading to effective preventive and remedial measures is the only solution to the problem. Failure to acknowledge the existence or the possibility of such a difficulty is extremely dangerous and constitutes a large step in the direction of encouraging divisiveness.

---

[2]Notice Paul's keen awareness of this in his comments in I Corinthians. But also do not fail to notice the use of multiple ministry in that congregation. Everything was not left to one man alone.

From the foregoing discussion, it may seem obvious that while there are advantages (fellowship, the power of specialization, etc.) there are also disadvantages to a multiple staff ministry. Perhaps the greatest is this: thinking that the addition of specialized staff members itself will serve the needs of a growingly large congregation. When "minister of music" (a dubious title), "of youth," and "of visitation," etc. are added, that does not necessarily mean that the congregation will be served better. If it is true that the ordinary pastor-teacher together with his elders cannot adequately minister to a congregation of more than 200 members in a truly shepherdly way (cf. John 10 and comments about knowing the names of the sheep and the voice of the shepherd), then when a congregation reaches the size of 800 or 1000 members, it still does not receive adequate *pastoral* work by the addition of a "minister of music" or a "minister of youth." What is needed is the addition of three or four more "ministers of sheep"! It is a rare congregation that sees this and sufficiently provides for the need. That is one reason why ordinarily it is better to start other congregations nearby rather than to allow a church to become too large (another reason stems from the use of the gifts of members: in a smaller congregation, as a rule, more of the members, in proportion, are called upon to use more of their gifts. Fellowship too, ordinarily, is closer in a smaller congregation). But where the emphasis is upon smaller congregations, provision also must be made for cooperation among these congregations in youth work, senior citizens work, etc. Otherwise, special groups in a congregation that has only a few such members tend to be neglected in the interest of the majority. Careful shepherdly concern is essential, therefore, in larger or smaller congregations, for it focuses not only on the 99, but also the hundredth sheep as well. When God's shepherds do not know each sheep "by name," and when they do not "know his voice" trouble is already on its way, whether the congregation is small or large. A church probably has grown too large when it becomes impossible to pray for those in need by name in the Sunday morning pastoral prayer. It is *adequate* pastoral work by the pastor-teacher and by the ruling elders that is the essential. Other matters, such as size, *per se,* are optional, and sometimes depend largely upon circumstances. There is no option about adequate shepherding. Whatever it takes to obtain it must be done; it is the one essential.

EXERCISE

For the Student or Pastor

Make a list of possible problems that may be encountered in a multiple staff ministry, together with possible solutions to each. If possible, interview men who hold such a relationship to each other for help.

Problems	Solutions

Problems	Solutions

CHAPTER SEVEN
CONGREGATIONAL MEETINGS

Congregational meetings in some churches have become the occasion for the annual church battle. Pent-up resentments, violent assertions of individual authority and rebellious protests against policies of the elders and/or pastor often characterize such gatherings. Sometimes, things said cut deeply into the unity of the congregation and leave lasting scars. Moreover, such meetings have been known to extend into the wee hours of the morning, with colossal amounts of time wasted, with thinning ranks indicating the frustration and disgust of many. All-in-all, the annual congregational meeting can be the darkest experience of the year.

It is necessary, therefore, by careful preparation, to guard against any such occurrences; not that all ill-will may be dispelled automatically thereby, but that at least it may be kept to a minimum. How may this be done? The basic answer lies in two areas: (1) prepare and conduct the meeting in such a way that expressions of bitterness become glaringly inappropriate; (2) if shepherdly care and discipline have been practiced properly during the year preceding, much (if not all) of the difficulty will be eliminated. Often, the existence of an annual protest meeting is dramatic evidence of the lack of such shepherdly concern. I should like to focus on the first of these two factors.

To begin with, much time can be saved by requiring that the reports of all organizations be mailed out to each home at least one week prior to the meeting. These may be compiled in one document together with an agenda and ought to carry a covering letter explaining that any questions of fact should be asked of the appropriate persons *before* the meeting. (Much time is wasted by members asking endless factual questions that should have been raised beforehand, outside of the meeting itself. It is not fair to the majority to allow this.) The moderator of the meeting should explain at the outset that there will be no time allowed for *such* discussion. This mailing also may include the new Church Directory. Like other meetings, not only an opening hour, but also a closing hour also should be announced

Members, then, can plan accordingly, and the business will be transacted with much more dispatch.

The meeting should be opened with the singing of a hymn, the Choir's favorite rendition of the year, and a ten minute message from the Word of God. A congregational fellowship supper preceding, allows more to attend and also helps to set a more relaxed tone of fellowship for the meeting. The moderator must exercise a fair but firm hand in conducting the meeting. At the outset, it is good for him to take 2-3 minutes to remind members of the basic rules of parliamentary procedure and to point out that remarks should be confined to issues, and must not be made about people. At the conclusion of the meeting (time should be allotted for this on the published agenda), time should be devoted to prayers of thanksgiving, confession, petition and commitment. Prayer especially may pertain to such matters as congregational losses/gains, projects undertaken at the meeting, etc.

Annual congregational meetings should be held, not in December or January, but in May. Since the Church year begins in September, it is wise to elect officers and initiate programs early enough to allow them to have the summer period for planning.

In preparing the pastor's report, it is helpful to look over the pastor's reports for the last two or three years. In this way, comparisons, trends, contrasts and changes may be noted. Such references may help both the pastor and the congregation to gain better perspective and to assess and gauge progress.[1] The report each year should present some *legitimate* challenge.

---

[1]The checklist in Appendix B may prove useful for pastors to review at this point. Perhaps it will provide a basis for some rough effort to be made during the ensuing year.

EXERCISE

For the Student

Interview at least three pastors and a dozen church members to discover what they think about congregational meetings. Focus on problems, possible solutions, improvements, etc. Report your findings to the class.

Notes

For the Pastor

1. In the space below, design a sample covering letter to be sent to the congregation announcing the Annual Congregational Meeting.

Cover Letter

2. Lay out a sample agenda for the congregational meeting.

Agenda

CHAPTER EIGHT
COMMUNICATION IN THE BODY

Much congregational management fails either from the lack of Christia communication or from its breakdown. A church that makes no attempt t promote Christian communication will discover that communication wi take place anyway. To state the problem simply: if the communication tha exists is not carefully established and maintained as *Christian* communica tion, then the sort of communication that develops will tend to be non Christian; gossip, slander, half truths will flow quickly along the grapevin The only effective way to assure against such perversions of truth is t develop and to maintain a vital communication network that, at ever point, scoops the grapevine. It must get the truth to each member soone more fully, more attractively, and with complete accuracy and honesty Therefore, it is important for every pastor to understand the principles c Christian communication and to learn how to promote it.

What is Christian communication and how may it be fostered? / fundamental passage concerning Christian communication within th church is found in Ephesians 4:25 (a verse that should be taken i conjunction with Ephesians 4:15):

> Therefore, laying aside falsehood, speak truth each one of you, with hi neighbor, for we are members of one another (v. 25),

and

> Speaking the truth in love, we are to grow up in all aspects into Him who is the head, even Christ (v. 15).

These two verses occur in the midst of a discussion of church unity an organization and as a prelude to discussions (in chapters 5,6) of clos functional relationships in the Church, the family and at work. Thes relationships, Paul makes clear, stand or fall on the basis of communica tion. His efforts to explain how Christian communication may b established and maintained, appearing as they do at this place, are intende to show that such communication is fundamental to any consideration of Christian unity, organization and function. It is of considerable importance, then, to discover what he has in mind.

There are at least four essential factors apparent in these two verses:

Christian Communication is Verbal

1. Communication, to be Christianly significant, to some extent must be verbal. That means that it may not be merely non verbal, or even largely written. When Paul wrote "speak truth each one of you with his neighbor," he had face-to-face communication in view. There are great advantages to face-to-face communication, especially when informing others about a change or decision that is likely to be unpopular or that readily may be misunderstood.[1] Written communication is more impersonal, the tone, emphasis and/or attitude of the writer may be missed entirely or misinterpreted. There are large benefits of voice and body in face-to-face communication that are missing from written communication. Moreover, the *reader* has no opportunity to pose questions, to request repetitions, to raise objections or to ask for examples. The *writer* is unable to adapt his presentation of data to such feedback. No wonder, then, in two sticky situations demanding the most of interpersonal contact the apostle John wrote:

> Having many things to write to you, I do not want to do so with paper and ink; but I hope to come to you and speak face to face, that your joy may be made full (II John 12).[2]

Clearly, actions may speak more loudly than words, but usually they do so less distinctly.[3] Frequently, there is a loss of precision when moving from verbal to non-verbal communication. But writing, at times, may be even less informative than some actions. Yet there *are* advantages to written

---

[1] In beginning a vital new Home Bible Study and Prayer program that would replace a tottering prayer meeting, the pastor of one congregation *personally* instructed six men appointed by the Elders who, in turn, *personally* confronted all of the heads of the households in the congregation about the program, answering all questions and extending an invitation to participate. What had to be accomplished was too important to entrust to impersonal written notices that were not equipped to handle feedback or give needed encouragement. The success of the program largely stemmed from this *personal* implementation.

[2] Cf. also III John 13,14. He is dealing with issues of heresy and of church discipline in these letters. Note Paul's desire for face-to-face communication expressed in Galatians 4:20. He was sure that personal contact would resolve the difficulties that now perplexed him concerning the Galatians.

[3] Actions may speak more loudly than words, but attitudes can outclass both: (1) Hand her a flower (action); (2) say "I love you" (words); (3) *lethargically* (attitude)! In good communication there is a harmony of the three. Attitudes are sensed or deduced from bodily states, vocal tones and/or word choice.

material just as there are advantages to each of the other modes: more care can be taken to word what one wants to say, diagrams and charts may be included, the material can be used for future reference, etc.

What then should a pastor's communication policy be? In communication with persons in the church, it is better not to rely solely upon impersonal written notices on the bulletin board, or in the monthly calendar, or in the Sunday bulletin. Usually, the best presentation is a combination of the written and spoken word that takes advantage of the values of both (and also, when appropriate involves non-verbal elements). Often the ideal way to present information is to introduce and explain it personally *from a mimeographed handout* which on that occasion may be distributed to the listeners. Overhead projectors, chalkboards and charts also may be used with profit when communicating with a group. Use of prepared material shows that thought and time has been given to the preparation of the presentation. This will make it clear that what you are saying was not dreamed up on the way to the meeting. People appreciate others taking time and effort to make such preparation.

Often, not only the manner,[4] but even the *context* in which difficult material is presented may be strongly determinative of the result. Difficult changes ought not to be presented in hurried, tense or pressured contexts. It is wise, frequently, to *develop* a proper context for such presentations (e.g., at a fellowship dinner or a men's breakfast called to consider the question).

Timing can be of great importance not only to preserve accuracy but also to assure a proper hearing for the message (presented in correct attitude, context, etc.). If the elders are planning to ask the church organist to allow someone else to share in the accompaniment of the congregational singing, but she learns this *from the newly acquired organist* before the elders get around to inquiring; or if the sunday school teachers hear that there will be a general change of the classrooms *from the grapevine* rather than from the Superintendent of the Church School, needless trouble can develop that otherwise might have been avoided by a proper presentation of the program *in context,[5] in person, in time.* Many of the aspects of proper communication really boil down to three things (1) showing consideration

---

[4]Such questions are of importance; cf. Colossians 4:3-6.

[5]Suppose the organist discovers the fact by coming to the church to practice on the organ only to find it already in use by the newly considered organist who is already at work practicing! Here is an obvious problem caused by poor communication.

for others, (2) doing what must be done right away and (3) courage to confront others.[6]

Christian Communication is Truthful

2. Communication, according to Ephesians 4:25 not only must be verbal, but it must be truthful. It is easy to avoid, to shade or to minimize the truth. None of us finds that it is easy to tell the truth under every circumstance. Indeed the concern for truth is a special matter for the Christian because for him even the old saw, "honesty is the best policy," is not true. For him, the sole answer can be that honesty is the only policy. It is not always necessary to tell all of the truth to everyone under every circumstance. Some issues need not be raised ("John you sure have a big nose") others may be sidestepped ("How do you like my new hat?" "Oh, it *is* new isn't it!"). Yet, in all of those matters in which information is necessary for the functioning of the whole body it is important to supply adequate, truthful information.

We have an interesting idea about truth; "the truth hurts" we often say. That saying shows how sinful men fear truth. It also indicates that truth has power. Of course the truth frequently hurts! No one likes to hear that his teaching in the youth group is unsatisfactory; yet he must be told so even though it hurts the teacher's feeling. No one likes to tell an elder that he is failing to serve Christ properly by his unwillingness to assume his responsibilities in the church; yet at times the pastor and the other elders must do so, even though it hurts them all to have to do it. So, it is true that the truth *hurts*.

But, that is not the whole story. The truth helps and the truth heals too. And, what is more, while the truth hurts, it never hurts like a lie. Falsehood among God's people can never help! Until Jane humbly confesses to him, "John I do not love you: I have never loved you — not when we were first married; not since. I married you on the rebound and principally for security; I have sinned and I am sorry," nothing can be done about their problem. Of course, it hurt both of them when she said this, but *now*, and only *now*, that the truth is out, can something be done about the matter.[7] Until she spoke the truth, he had known something was wrong but never could decide what. He tried many times to find out, worried about what he

---

[6]One of the last times to opt for written communication over the spoken is when you are afraid to face another, or suspect that he might think you are. It is easy to rationalize turning to the written page at this point by saying "I can be more precise," etc. Cf. the charge of Paul's opponents and his response in II Corinthians 10:1-11.

[7]Sooner or later, in this life or in the next, the truth about every man will be made public (cf. I Timothy 5:24,25).

could do, blamed himself; all to no avail.[8] Now, she had hurt him by telling him the truth, but it was not like the hurt of not knowing — always sure something was between them, but always guessing about what it might be. Now, she had hurt him like the physician, who hurts in order to heal. This is the hurt of love; indeed, by risking his wrath, his rejection, or whatever response might be forthcoming, she had taken the first step of love toward him.

Not only could something now be done about the problem since at last John had the truth rather than guesses to work with, but the old hurts could vanish. For years the hurts that came from his faulty responses and fears, combined with his ignorance of the true situation and inability to cope with the unknown, continually had plagued them both. Now he could put aside his guesses and wrong responses and together they could move ahead constructively as God would have them, to face the *facts*.

On every level, in the home, in counseling, in the many interpersonal conflicts that arise in the course of the organizational functioning of the body, truth is the vital fluid that oils the machinery to keep it moving freely. Always, it must be applied liberally in order to keep down the heat that arises from friction! Which leads us to the third factor.

Christian Communication is Adequate

3. God not only requires personal, truthful communication when He commands "speak truth each one of you with his neighbor," but from this verse it is plain that He demands adequate communication as well. It is not enough for *some* to speak the truth; *each one* must do so; and he must communicate to *all* of those who function closely with him (i.e., his neighbors). People must not be taken for granted. One way to be certain not to do so is to be sure that you give everyone all of the data that he needs in order to function properly in coordination with you and with others in the body. That, of course, demands thoughtfulness and concern about the other person. It means pulling *his* socks on and viewing the whole from *his* perspective.

Take an example drawn from the figure that underlies the reason that Paul appends: "for we are members one of another"; the figure of the body. Elsewhere in the chapter[9] and in I Corinthians[10] the same figure is worked

---

[8]Of course these responses on his part were not proper either and may have made it more difficult for John's wife to tell him the truth.

[9]V. 16. N.B., there Paul clearly observes that it is "speaking the truth in love" (v. 15) that makes such bodily coordination possible.

[10]I Corinthians 12:12ff.

out in more detail. The point is made that all of the parts are necessary; indeed all are necessary to one another and, of course, to manifest the *fullness* of Christ. Here, in v. 25, Paul observes that it is necessary to speak adequate truth in order to establish and maintain good coordination within the body. If the hand and arm have one set of data, while the knees and legs do not, the knees may bend and the body may attempt to sit down just as the hand reaches around and pulls the chair out from beneath. Ludicrous! Yes, but no more so than the tragic ways in which members of the same body work at cross purposes, duplicate efforts unnecessarily, and (in general) fail to coordinate activities in the local congregation.

It is the pastor's job, even as Paul considered it his, to see to it that such breakdown of harmony does not result from inadequate communication. For instance, there is *no excuse* for two groups to plan for conflicting meetings on the same dates if an adequate system of communication has been developed.[11] Communication between individuals and between groups must be encouraged and ways and means for assuring it must be devised. It is the pastor's duty to see to it that proper channels are developed, kept clear, and used. He *may* delegate the task (or portions of it — e.g., a telephone pyramid chain),[12] but must never so remove himself from concern with communication that he does not know at all times precisely what sort of communication exists. "How can you find out, you ask?" The very asking of the question by the pastor of a church demonstrates the need for better communication. Were communication what it should be, he would be receiving steady feedback about communication as well as about everything else. If nothing more, he can begin by using the old hat trick. It is very simple: he puts on his hat and goes out and polls a representative group of persons from his congregation (of course, at times, but not always, he could easily delegate *this* task too). He asks questions like, "Did you hear about the last five announcements we made? How did you hear? Do you have any suggestions for getting information to our membership more rapidly? More precisely? Actually, a good feedback system may be built by appointing sampler reporters. Ten or so persons, in sample situations (a shut-in, a young person, a travelling

---

[11]For such matters, a monthly calendar on which all dates of activities are entered, and which is published or posted and accessible to all members and groups at all times, could forestall such problems. The pastor may readily hand over the task of devising and maintaining such a system to his diaconate.

[12]The chain is simple and effective. The pastor calls deacon Smith who calls three others, who call three others, etc. until all members have been reached. Emergency prayer requests, last minute announcements, cancellation of meetings, births, deaths, causes for congregational rejoicing and thanksgiving, etc., may be phoned down the chain. The setting up and maintenance of the chain may be left to the diaconate.

salesman, etc.) report once each month on how well communication is functioning.

So, to sum up so far, we have seen that spoken, truthful and adequate communication is essential for the coordination and proper functioning of the congregation.

Christian Communication is Loving

4. But, now notice that the fourth element, prominently mentioned in v. 15, is *love*. Communication not only allows for the movement of data back and forth along the lines,[13] thus providing the proper conditions for coordination, but proper communication also enables the sheep in the flock to develop and to maintain good relations with the Chief Shepherd, His undershepherds, and with one another. Communication provides the setting that fosters brotherly love, and (cyclically) it is brotherly love that fosters good communication. Thus communication is the precondition for the spread and maintenance of Christian love, even as love is also the precondition for speaking the truth. Truth without love becomes a wicked weapon. Love, uncommunicated, is a blunted blessing.

Always, therefore, in endeavoring to further communication, the pastor must be concerned about maintaining good relationships in the body through love. That means that temper and resentment, the two foes of good communication mentioned in Ephesians 4, must be handled. Both temper and resentment close down communication. I do not want to develop this

---

[13] And one must be sure that the communication network in the congregation does operate in *both* directions; otherwise something less than *adequate* communication is taking place.

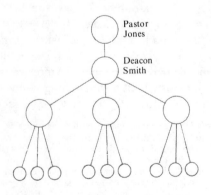

point further since I have said much about it already in other places.[14] Here, let me add only this: in the context of Ephesians 4:25, as Paul continues to discuss communication, he definitively disposes of these twin evils by showing that when held in or ventillated with abandon, anger becomes sin. Only when released under control, and aimed at problems, not persons, may one "be angry yet not sin." The pastor's task is to see to it that sinful manifestations of anger do not block communication within the church.

Because Christians nevertheless are still sinners, rubs will come. Many will be "covered" in love. But some keep throwing the covers off. There is a great necessity for teaching members how to deal with them when they do. Unless the problems that sinners cause by their sinful attitudes and actions are handled in a biblical manner, they will disrupt the orderly work of the congregation.[15] As James put it, "where jealousy and selfish ambition exist, there is disorder and every evil thing" (James 3:16). This is a matter of vital concern to a leader; whatever causes disorder in the flock must be dealt with quickly and effectively. Moreover, the pastor must see to it not only that they understand them, but that members put to work these biblical principles for dealing with difficulties.

An example of the need for such a face-to-face confrontation in the case of unresolved anger is recorded in Philippians 4:1,2 where Paul not only exhorts Euodia and Syntyche to "be of one mind in the Lord," but then goes on to urge the pastor[16] to step in to be sure that reconciliation is effected:

> Indeed, true comrade,[17] I ask you to help those women who have shared my struggle in the gospel together with Clement also....

Plainly, Paul determined to put an end to the contention in the church. He was concerned to bring about the reconciliation of persons who formerly had proven to be able to work together with him and with one another courageously in the service of Christ. But because of some difficulty (we are not told what) Euodia and Syntyche (and possibly others with them) had fallen out with one another. Presumably, *because in the process,*

---

[14]Cf. *Christian Living in the Home,* Chapter Three, *The Christian Counselor's Manual,* pp. 250,322,362ff. I should like also to mention the strong effects of fear in blocking communication.

[15]Cf. *The Christian Counselor's Manual,* pp. 52,359 for a fuller discussion of love covering a multitude of sins.

[16]It is true that the word *suzuge* could be read as a name, Syzygos, but there is no evidence, in the Scriptures or elsewhere, that such a name existed. It is better, therefore, to take the comment to refer to the pastor who was, doubtless, reading the letter to the congregation.

[17]Literally, "fellow yoke-bearer—a term describing one who worked jointly with him in Christ's ministry.

communication had broken down, Paul not only exhorts them to be reconciled, but also urges the pastor to get involved. He knew that there was only one way to solve the communication dilemma[18] to enlist the help and counsel of another. The pastor must be ready to trouble shoot whenever he sees a communication breakdown leading to unsettled differences among the members of his congregation. Such help is needed in every circumstance where a brother or sister on his own does not find his way out of his sin (cf. especially Galatians 6:1ff.).

Pastors, then, must be alive both to the possibilities provided by proper Christian communication and to the problems that may arise from its breakdown, nonexistence or the admixture of nonchristian elements. In no case may they ignore the potential of communication (good or bad), for by it the life of the congregation is maintained.

Interpersonal Relations and Differences

Administration in the church bogs down significantly when the pastor himself does not know how to establish and maintain proper relationships with those with whom he must work. And even when he does, the work of the congregation will suffer if he fails to teach others how to do so. Of course all aspects of his ministry are affected adversely when he is incompetent in Christian personal relations.

Good administration requires courage and skill coupled with love and concern in *confronting* people about their differences. I begin by putting the stress here because it should go without saying that the pastor must discover and pursue every legitimate avenue open to him to keep relations on a high Christian plane and to prevent their breakdown at all costs. Many men make good attempts preventively, but utterly fail when they must confront those who have gone astray. No matter how skilled he may become in preventive activities, no matter how well the pastor has been able to avoid innumerable conflicts by wise policy, the inevitable will happen: sinners will differ in sinful and unpleasant ways which, if left unchecked, will destroy not only their own lives, but the witness and productivity of Christ's church. Therefore, it is particularly necessary to encourage pastors to take biblical action when differences arise among the people of God.

I say that it takes courage to confront others at such times. Unfortunately, many pastors lack such courage. Timothy had to be exhorted by the apostle Paul to be more courageous in his ministry (I Timothy 4:12, II Timothy 1:6-8). "Fine," you say, "I wish I *were* more

---

[18]The communication dilemma is this: Communication is necessary to solve problems between persons, including the communication problem!

courageous, but I'm not. How do I become so; is there any hope?" Yes there is. Courage is, as Paul says, *developed;* it does not appear full-grown. Courage comes, not by sitting around praying for it, or waiting for it to come; that is not what the apostle advised Timothy. Rather, courage comes when a pastor recognizes the will of God in the Scriptures, determines that by God's grace he will do whatever he knows that God requires of him, and prayerfully sets out to obey, whether he *feels* courageous or not. If the courage does not come in the doing the first time around, he will find at length, as he continues to follow God's will again and again, that God will develop courage in him. Changes do not ordinarily come instantly between 1:00 A.M. and 1:01 A.M. on Thursday; they take time to develop through the obedient pursuit of biblical practices.

Pastors must not allow personal differences among members of the flock to fester and harden (Ephesians 4:26; Philippians 4:2,3). When they do, these differences will crystallize into bitterness and resentment. Whenever the possibility for this exists the wise pastor will anticipate it and warn against that eventuality. For instance, when he suspects that a heated debate might be likely to occur in a committee meeting, he will take time at the outset to caution against allowing differences of opinion to grow into differences of relationship. He will instruct the committee members to be careful about *how* they differ (choice of words, tone of voice, volume, etc.). He also will pray for a good outcome. He will continually stress the need for members to express their differences regarding their interpretations and applications of the Scriptures, but he will emphasize also that their differences of opinion must not be allowed to become personal differences. By his own behavior, he will endeavor to so set the tone of the meeting. He will see to it that the expression of different viewpoints is never stifled, but also that personal hostilities are minimized. That is part of his job as an officer of the church given to help the members of the church to grow together into the *unity* of the faith in *love* (cf. Ephesians 4:1-16).

The pastor, as a model in all things, must set a good example himself. He must encourage the honest expression of disagreement with his own opinions and must not allow it to get between him and any member of his congregation. Members will best learn how to differ as Christians from observing his own practice. Yet, it is right here that many pastors fail. They become saddened, sit and stew in self pity and even get depressed because they have been challenged by a member of the congregation. A careful review of the qualities of the overseer in Titus 1:7, 8 makes it clear that he may not follow any such course. Instead, a pastor (who should always be alert for ways to teach the flock) should seize upon the occasion as an opportunity to *demonstrate* the truth he has been teaching verbally. Attitudes, and those actions that grow out of them, often are best conveyed through such informal channels; on the other hand, information usually is best channeled through more formal ones.

The pastor also must learn (by prayerful, committed effort) how to differ, rebuke and encourage in love if he would become an effective leader (cf. especially II Timothy 2:24,25). Some can handle the differences that are expressed against their viewpoint quite well, but they themselves have great difficulty differing with another. And they are the ones who usually find the task of rebuking especially hard. But leadership at times requires doing difficult things such as telling someone he has sinned, and must repent, or that his services no longer are desired in a certain position. Leadership may demand that he confront a church school teacher or a sexton who has been slack in his work. Of course, not every confrontation of this sort should be made by the pastor (too frequently it is assumed that it is solely his job); the elders and the deacons and the other leaders of the congregation also must learn how to handle such situations. But if they have never done so before, or if they have not yet learned to do so well, from time to time the pastor will find it necessary to step in as a trouble shooter and a model, taking the elder or deacon along as he shows him how it is done. The presence of an elder or deacon, besides providing him with the needed experience, can be a plus factor in the confrontation itself. His presence can steady the discussion, keep it from becoming personalized and provide a witness to what was said and done. Indeed, at times the pastor might need one.

One of the most dissatisfying and disheartening things that can happen in a church is for members to sense that there is an underlying tension between the participants in meetings as they try to work together. It throws a wet blanket over everyone's spirit. This tension is due almost always to unresolved difficulties. It is important, therefore, for the pastor not only to preach about such matters, but periodically to give talks and lectures to the members of each organization in the congregation about the proper means of working together for the honor of Christ. And there are times when he must take various members aside and talk to them about their relationship to one another and how it is affecting the ministry of the congregation. He may never allow anything that he sees to be hindering the effective working of the body to continue to hamper the work of Christ. Probably more churches are split (or go limping along) because of interpersonal differences that were not dealt with biblically than because of doctrinal disagreements. Much power is drained off and enormous amounts of energy are wasted in unnecessary tension and misery arising from mishandled conflicts. The pastor must be vigilant to follow the directions given in Matthew 18, Matthew 5, Luke 17, Ephesians 4 and the principles of other key passages that insist upon the speedy and full resolution of all personal differences between God's people.[19] As he does so, he will become the prime example and living embodiment of the reconciliation/discipline dynamic (cf., especially, the Chapter of that name in *The Christian Counselor's Manual* for details on how to do this).

EXERCISE

For the Student and the Pastor

Diagram the lines of communication that actually exist in your (another) congregation.

---

[19]Cf. *Competent to Counsel* and *The Christian Counselor's Manual* for detailed discussions f these passages.

CHAPTER NINE
COMMUNICATION LINKS

Let us now consider some of the varieties of communication links that might be formed to move information back and forth from the pastor (and other officers of the church) and from the members of the congregation.

1. *Weekly announcements* may be given from the pulpit and in the church bulletin. Not every announcement in the bulletin should also be announced from the pulpit. However, whenever there are announcements not made audibly, it is wise to indicate the fact by saying "For further announcements consult the bulletin," or words to that effect.[1] Bulletins should be prepared under the guidance of the deacons, who may act, in most publicity and informational capacities, as a liaison between the pastor and the members of the congregation.[2]

2. *A monthly newspaper* (including a monthly calendar of events) is an extremely valuable asset to any congregation. As in the case of the bulletin, it should be edited by a responsible person (usually one of the ordained office bearers is desirable) who will be able to make wise judgments about what should (or should not) be included, when to alter wording, etc. Here, in this paper, budding young (or old) writers have an opportunity to serve Christ by means of their pens. Always, there should be a shut-ins section, *written by* and distributed to them. Older members, who may be making

---

[1] Some think that announcements of church affairs do not constitute a worthy part of the worship service. I disagree. If it is worthy to be done by the church, it is worthy to be announced. No artificial, unbiblical dichotomy between doing the Lord's work and the worship of God ought to be held. A study of the New Testament terms *latreia* and *leitourgia* provides an interesting commentary on the question. They show that worship and service are inextricably bound up in one another.

[2] Much more may be said about bulletins. Later, in a subsequent volume, I plan to discuss some liturgical matters concerning the order of worship but here I refer only to the second page of the bulletin. In discussing written communication, it is of importance to note that the pastor should *never* get involved in the mechanical affairs of production. Too many pastors busy themselves with repairing mimeograph machines when they ought to be repairing marriages. The pastor should keep a file of bulletins for his own future reference. He will be surprised how often this reference source will provide needed information. A second file, bound, should be placed in the church library.

the transition from the first phase of their lives to a second,[3] may wish to take the opportunity to write. This monthly paper should be mailed to those not present on the day of its distribution,[4] to servicemen, students at college, and persons who have visited previously. An extra supply, for guests and for members who wish to distribute them to friends and neighbors ought to be made available.[5] This should be encouraged through the various channels of communication.

A standard, printed cover, in color (I suggest warm colors: oranges, reds, yellows), will give added attractiveness to the paper. There ought to be sections devoted to calendar and general news, to children, to youth, to the infirm and shut-ins, to the family, to a daily prayer calendar (for members, missionaries, needs), to Christian fiction, etc., each of which may be mimeographed on different colored paper stock to easily distinguish them. In general, color attracts more than white and black. These papers should be bound and filed in the church library for future reference. You will be surprised at how often you too will turn to your own bound set for various reasons.

3. *Bulletin boards, charts, graphs, posters* provide a useful means for announcing events, posting missionary letters (which when taken from the board may be bound in the congregational missionary scrap book and placed in the library),[6] reminding members of the church library (announcing new acquisitions, etc.), and dozens of other purposes.[7] It is vital to have several boards, placed in strategic locations where those who are concerned about the information that they contain may easily see them. One general board causes crowding, allows for little creativity in terms of posters and other art work, and discourages use. It is essential for each board to be reviewed and updated *weekly*. Ratty, soiled notices, containing dated materials communicate too; but what they say to guests is not what

---

[3]Cf. *Shepherding God's Flock,* Vol. II, pp. 104-113.

[4]This implies that a careful record of attendance is kept. Attendance records are vital as well for good pastoral care. Several methods are in use: (1) Passing an attendance record sign-up sheet or book, (2) Depositing a card in the offering plate (or a box at the rear of the church building), or (3) The plain old usher count (the ushers have lists of families and simply look over the congregation and mark off those present and those absent).

[5]Mailing lists should be checked by a person assigned to weed out dead addresses at least quarterly, but especially to be sure that all new ones have been added.

[6]These will be found useful for later missionary programs, studies, talks, etc.

[7]A photograph report of last year's summer camping experience on the Young People's board will probably encourage more to attend this year than bland announcements in writing or even the full color brochure published by the camp. Yet, in all such good things, someone must be made responsible to take the pictures *with this in mind* (other shots by participants also could be included) and then someone also must be responsible for arranging these in a display, or it will not come off well.

we should want to communicate. The only way to be sure that each board is properly cared for is to make someone associated with it responsible for it, and to make someone responsible for checking on his work (not in a censorious, but in a helpful and encouraging manner).

4. *Tapes (audio and video),* and sometimes mimeographed or printed transcriptions of these, become a useful adjunct to the other teaching ministries of a congregation. Shut-ins, and others at a distance, may profit from a weekly diaconal tape ministry faithfully carried out.[8] However, the Christian Church has only *begun* to utilize tapes. Cheap, portable and dependable, these recorders can be employed in Christ's service in many ways.[9] For instance, one member of the congregational teaching staff may be sent to an important conference or lecture with the expressed purpose of taping and then playing the tape(s) at discussion groups planned for this purpose. Missionaries and congregations, through cassette, can draw nearer. Youth groups can plan and produce programs to be exchanged with other youth groups. A tape library should be built up by each congregation. A tape deck (that plays, but does not record, i.e., does not erase tapes) should be provided by the library to assure the safety of the tapes. It is possible to tape planning meetings (or those portions of them that would be valuable to the members of the planning group or to others later on). These, then may be circulated among the participants for further reflection. Reports of individuals or of committees, may be prepared ahead of time on tape and brought (or even sent) to members of the larger body. Vast vistas of creative use of the cassette yet lie immediately ahead.

5. *Telephone and telephone chains*[10] quickly deliver emergency, crucial or last minute information.[11] By use of the telephone, one may reach out beyond the congregation and even extend a contact as far as the mission field. A personal phone conversation with a home or foreign missionary (taped, or amplified and played live) at a prayer meeting or missionary conference will add a vital dimension.[12] Prayer, for someone rushed to the hospital in critical condition on Thursday, should not wait for Sunday or

---

[8]Cf. *Shepherding God's Flock,* Vol. I, pp. 126,127.

[9]Cassettes are now universal. The time may be coming when video cassettes will be almost as accessible to us. Creativity is needed to exploit the full range of possibilities that cassette tapes provide for communication.

[10]Cf. *supra.*

[11]Including, as Mick Knierim, one of my students rightly pointed out, matters of *praise* as well as other matters. But do not *overuse* the chain or (1) it will soon breakdown; (2) it will lose its power to give special significance to a message.

[12]Rather than chase furloughed missionaries all over the map (especially during those years when their teenage children need them at home) congregations with profit could arrange for two or three amplified phone calls from the missionary and his family on prayer meeting nights. Gasoline, food and lodging are far more expensive than phone calls!

for next week's Wednesday night prayer meeting. The request for prayer may be sent down the telephone chain so that, frequently, the entire congregation can be alerted to pray within a few hours.[13] The telephone is an invaluable timesaver when used wisely and considerately. Much business, that otherwise would take people from their homes to attend meetings, can be carried on by way of a conference call. Use of the conference call, in the long run, is more economical and certainly less time consuming. It best may be used for urgent or last minute decision-making, providing new information, matters requiring only brief discussion, and brief reporting. Many pastors do not use their phones often enough.

6. *Face-to-face contacts of all sorts,* nevertheless, must remain the fundamental and bread-and-butter means for conveying information. Regular meetings are essential for this purpose. But most meetings last too long because they are conducted poorly (irrelevant discussion may preponderate),[14] because insufficient individual tasks have been assigned previously (people come unprepared to report and to discuss), and because a closing hour has not been set. Some of the other five suggestions mentioned previously may help to slim down regular meetings.[15] Pastors must not forget that much of the best communication takes place informally between persons invited to regular meetings. Therefore, the basic rule should be: keep the meeting itself brief and schedule a fellowship time in conjunction with it (a meal or a snack often provides the necessary context for informal discussion). It is especially important to provide for such informal fellowship among persons who must meet and work together regularly, even if little or no task-oriented communication takes place since it provides further opportunities for them to develop the good personal relationships that are essential to clear channels of communication.

---

[13]One congregation has no regular prayer meeting, but members meet at the church (as they are able) upon request. They may meet any time of day according to needs. The pastor of this church reports more vital prayer and greater attendance then before. Prayer for regular needs is encouraged in various groups and in the family.

[14]This sort of discussion should be postponed to the informal coffee-and-doughnut period that follows (or interrupts; the interrupting fellowship time assures full participation. The one that follows the meeting allows some to slip off more quickly for home).

[15]Slimmed down meetings are desirable whenever possible. Communication is not improved by more words; it is productive words alone that count.

EXERCISE

For the Student

Together with a group of four or five other students, produce a simulated monthly newspaper. Try to think through creative and interesting ways of presenting the material.

For the Pastor

Check out the congregational communication links mentioned in this chapter (together with others you may have developed) to determine how well they are functioning.

CHAPTER TEN
ENLISTING AND TRAINING

A full discussion of the individual gifts of members cannot be carried on here with any sort of adequacy. Yet there are some fundamental factors that are relevant to the matter of enlisting and training members of the flock for their work of ministry that should be considered.

First, notice that these gifts of the Spirit are *that,* and exactly that—gifts. They are not rewards given to those Christians who earn or deserve them by the so-called "spirituality"[1] of their lives. No congregation of Christians mentioned in the New Testament was more unsanctified in doctrine and life than the Corinthian Church, yet gifts were given to that congregation in *fullness.* (Paul wrote: "You are not lacking in any gift," I Corinthians 1:7.) It is clear, then, that the gifts of the Spirit are *gifts* graciously dispensed; nothing more, nothing less. They are distributed sovereignly by the Spirit, as He wills, according to the measure determined by Him, for His own inscrutable purposes (cf. Ephesians 4:7; I Corinthians 12:4-7: 11b). They are neither earned nor merited.

We are not told explicitly *when* God imparts gifts to His children, but since they are said to be Spiritual gifts, they are to be thought of not as natural talents, but as abilities given (probably at the new birth, concurrent with the Spirit's coming into each life)[2] in addition to those natural capacities given at the first, or physical birth. Of course these gifts might include a heightening of natural talents.

The extraordinary, or apostolic gifts, however, were given later, by the laying on of the hands of the apostles, to *confirm* their apostolic witness and word (cf. II Corinthians 12:12; I Corinthians 1:6; Hebrews 2:2-4; Acts 8:14-20; 19:6). If the miraculous gifts could come to any and to all believers

---

[1]Such use of the term spirituality is inaccurate and disturbing. It stresses human merit when all that is spiritual is the work (fruit) of the Spirit.

[2]However, the special, extraordinary gifts clearly are marked out as given at a later point (cf. Rom. 1:11; I Corinthians 14:13; II Timothy 6:1, etc.).

in any other way,[3] they would not be the "signs of an apostle" (II Corinthians 12:12), nor would they "confirm" (Hebrews 2:3,4) God's revelatory words spoken and written by the apostles or under their supervision. If every Christian could obtain the miraculous sign-gifts from a source other than from the apostles, then such gifts would be the signs of a *Christian,* and not as Paul claimed, the signs of an *apostle.*

The officers of the church, listed in Ephesians 4, plainly are divided into two groups: (1) *apostles and prophets,* whose temporary functions, in the same book, are called "foundational" (cf. Ephesians 2:20; 3:3-5); (2) *evangelists (missionaries) and pastor-teachers* whose work continues perpetually in the church. As these two kinds of offices (special and ordinary) existed in the early church,[4] so too there were two distinct sorts of gifts: (1) *special,* "confirmation" or "sign" gifts, that came to believers through the apostles; (2) *ordinary,* "service" gifts, that came to believers directly from the Spirit. We shall speak in this section, then, only of those ordinary gifts given by God to enable His Church in any age to function and to carry on its many ministries.

Next, let us recognize that *every* Christian has gifts (cf. Ephesians 4:7, "to each one of us..." and I Peter 4:10, "as each one has received a gift..." and I Corinthians 12:11, ". . .distributing to each one individually"). All Christians, therefore, must be encouraged to find a place of usefulness in ministering to others. It is the pastor's task not only to preach and teach this fact, but (in addition) to help each individual to discover, develop and deploy his gift. The pastor must remember that, according to Ephesians 4:12, it is the object of his shepherding ministry to equip each sheep to minister. Recruiting and enlisting Christians for those ministries that accord with their gifts then, is, a fundamental and first task of pastoral leadership. In a course of study for new converts (and/or for others who need the instruction) one of the prime concerns of the pastor or elder who teaches it is to instruct those who attend about gifts. At the conclusion of the course, hopefully, most of those who have attended should know at least in what possible areas their gifts may lie and should be prepared to test

---

[3]Of course, in the two great outpourings of Pentecost (Acts 2) and the gentile pentecost Acts 10) the confirmation, or sign gifts were given directly, signifying the *immediate* coming of the Spirit. But in the two spill-overs from each of these outpourings (Acts 8; Acts 19), the apostles gave the Spirit (with His gifts) by the laying on of hands *mediately.*

[4]Also called "gifts" (Ephesians 4:8,11). The officers were men gifted for their work as well as Christ's gift to His Church. Both ideas seem to be in the apostle's mind as he writes in Ephesians 4. They were gifted gifts.

their gifts by being directed into tasks in the congregation that belong to those areas.[5].

The teacher of such a course may wish to develop a program based upon Romans 12:3-7 in which the framework for such a discussion may be found:

Evaluation

1. Every member must be taught to evaluate his life soberly in order to discover God's gifts (v. 3). And in doing so, he must not think more highly of himself than he ought to think. On the other hand, sober judgment demands no by-passing or underestimating of the gifts of God. One is to evaluate the "measure of faith" allotted to himself. The phrase "measure of faith" is peculiar. Instead one might expect to read words like "varieties of gifts" or "particular tasks." Clearly, that is what Paul is referring to, the allotment of distinct gifts for particular ministries. But, why then, does he use this expression instead? To what does he refer when he speaks of "a measure, or portion, of faith"? Murray thinks that the distinct endowments variously distributed to believers, each receiving his own measure, are called measures of faith in order to "emphasize the cardinal place which faith occupies...in the specific functions performed."[6]

Coordination

2. He must recognize the place and the function of his individual gift in the body (vv. 4,5). He, together with other believers, must function as part of a whole. Recognizing his place, its relation to the whole and the place and function of others will help him to think more highly of himself but also to see the essential contribution that the exercise of his gift makes to all. He will recognize both his dependence upon others and their dependence upon him. Paul, in his great Declaration of Interdependence, puts it this way:

> Just as we have many members in one body and all the members do not have the same function, so we, who are many, are one body in Christ, and individually members one of another (Romans 12:4,5).

So then, first, the pastor must help each member to make a sober judgment

---

[5]In examining possible gifts, the lists given by Paul may be used with profit as suggestive of what spiritual gifts are like, but should not be thought to be exhaustive any more than the other lists that Paul gives elsewhere in his letters.

[6]John Murray, *The Epistle to the Romans*, Vol. II (Wm. B. Eerdmans Pub. Co., Grand Rapids: 1965), p. 119. Cf. also the use of the word "measure" in II Corinthians 10:13.

about his gifts; after that it is important for him to help each one to gain a recognition of the place and purpose of that gift in the work of the whole congregation. This will steer a course around any temptations to develop lone wolf attitudes, or (on the other extreme) to think one's ministry is irrelevant. But there is one more step necessary.

Participation

3. Each member, having soberly taken stock of his gifts, and having recognized where he fits into the big picture, must in fact begin to take on tasks in the area or areas of his gifts and begin to function as a contributing part of the body. This is what Paul has in mind in verse 6:

> And since we have gifts that differ according to the grace given to us, let us exercise them accordingly....

The pastor will be concerned about helping every Christian in the congregation to discover, to develop and to *deploy* his gifts.

Not everything can be done at once. Gifts may become growingly useful, or may atrophy through disuse; they may be used properly for scriptural ends, or may be misused for sinful ends.[7] They may be used selfishly or, as intended, for the benefit of all. Therefore, the development of the gifts of the members of the body through instruction, putting them to use, encouragment and critique, are all matters that should be of great concern to the pastor. The pastor will see to it that he introduces a new Christian into ministry slowly; he will be sure that he does not subject him to unnecessary temptations toward pride, by recognizing his novice status. With reference to elders Paul writes, "not a new convert, lest he become conceited and fall into the condemnation of the devil" (I Timothy 3:6). He will be zealous to follow Paul's directions in I Timothy 5:22: "Do not lay hands on anyone too hastily." If he seems to possess qualities that may be used in the eldership or diaconate, the pastor will wait to be sure before encouraging ordination and, instead, will insist first that he be tested (I Timothy 3:10; II Corinthians 8:22). The same principles apply, of course, to any member of the congregation using any gifts. No one can at first accomplish what he can produce only by subsequent study and experience.

How does this turn out in practice? Perhaps Fred possesses gifts that would seem to point toward the diaconate. Paul says "let him be tested first" (I Timothy 3:10). Since gifts are not the only factor to consider (such matters as one's faithfulness in using them, not to speak of his attitude or the ends for which he uses his gifts, are relevant factors too), the pastor will

---

[7] Cf. the misuse of spiritual gifts in Corinth.

be interested in putting Fred into circumstances that will test out not only his gifts, but also his faithfulness, his fervency, his humility, his willingness, his capacity for working with others, etc. He may be asked to usher, to do auditing of the church books, etc. If he performs well in these tasks, others may be given, until it is clear to all that he is ready, able and willing to serve God in the larger capacity as a deacon.

Volunteers

How does one ask another to take on a task? There is no indication in the New Testament that persons were asked to volunteer. Asking for volunteer Church School teachers, for instance, is one sure way to destroy the teaching quality of the school. Moreover, it brings on all sorts of unwanted problems arising from the willingness of persons to serve who have neither the gifts nor other essential qualities for serving well. Instead, after testing several likely persons in other or in similar tasks (have them teach for a period every now and then as a substitute, etc.), and after agreement by the members of the board of elders, the person chosen should be appointed to the task, then told so by the pastor and/or another elder. He should not be *asked* if he will serve, but should rather be told that he is the man (woman) that they want for this task. While reasonable causes for declination should be honored (the man truly does not have the time *now* to do this because of certain previously unknown family matters),[8] if less weighty reasons are adduced, the pastor should press the appointment by challenging him to enter into the opportunity (which should be spelled out specifically along with the obligations and duties involved) and stress the need of the whole body for his ministry. Unless truly weighty reasons are forthcoming, the pastor should refuse to take no for an answer.

It is important too to offer adequate help, resources, guidance and training, and the offer should be genuine and concrete. ("Bill, I've already arranged for Tom to spend the next six weeks taking you along with him as he distributes the tapes to the shut-ins and ministers to them. Then, he promises to remain on call at any time to be of help in sticky situations, and to counsel with you about any aspect of the work.") At some point, every member of the congregation, who is not already serving, should be approached in this manner about a ministry in which he or she may engage, whether it is teaching or ushering, providing transportation for a poor widow to attend church or taking on some aspect of the youth work.[9]

---

[8]But, before appointing him, it is important to take all such matters into consideration so far as they *are* known.

[9]But shun like the plague that all too frequently given (but totally unsavory) advice to offe jobs to unbelievers "in order to get them interested in the church."

The person enlisted should be given a clear picture of the purpose for which he has been enlisted. I did not say a job description, because that (as necessary as it may be) puts the emphasis in the wrong place. You do not enlist someone "to teach" or "to take the young people's group." The stress of the appointment should be upon some purpose or purposes that are in view: "to get the young people interested in serving Christ" or "to teach the nursery class that they come to church to find out about Jesus," or "to help the young couples to have happier marriages." It is not a job description only, but also a job *accomplishment* that you want to convey by your remarks. Your stress should not be upon function but upon purpose; not so much how (that must come later) but rather upon what.

In approaching persons with gifts that seem to be directed toward service in a particular area, the pastor must remember that not *every* task in that area may be pursued as well by every person who has gifts that are appropriate to the area. That is to say, gifts differ not only in kind, but also in purpose *and* results. Listen to the following:

> Now there are varieties of gifts... varieties of ministries, and... varieties of effects (I Corinthians 12:4-6). These gifts differ also "according to the measure of Christ's gift" (Ephesians 4:7).

It is wrong to place persons in positions that demand more than they have the capabilities to deliver, or on the other hand, to cramp them with jobs too small to fit them. Nor is it right to allow persons to remain in tasks whose skins they have burst.[10] In the latter case, either they must be moved on to a larger work since they have outgrown the previous task, or the job in which they have been laboring must be enlarged to fit them.

Differing measures of the same gift will result in somewhat differing results. Comparisons with others are particularly odious in the light of this fact. Therefore, it is important for the pastor to help each man to find a task (1) in the area of his gifts, (2) that fits the measure of his capacities, and (3) to challenge him to work in it to *his* fullest capacity.[11]

Finally, notice the basic short term purpose (on the long term, the purpose always is to honor God: I Peter 4:11b) of these gifts:

> ...to each one is given...for the common good (I Corinthians 12:7; cf. also vv. 14-31).

nd,

---

[10] Tasks should be reviewed regularly. What satisfied a person a year ago, today may be bad ewardship of his labors and thus no longer may bring a sense of achievement.

[11] That will not be the same as the capacity of another.

As each one has received a gift, employ it in serving one another, as good stewards of the manifold grace of God (I Peter 4:10).

Gifts are given in order to bring about the mutual ministry of each believer to all of the others in the body. No Christian, therefore, can be happy in his Christian experience until he knows that in some way he is doing something with his gifts, and that what he is doing is bringing blessing and help to other Christians. No pastor may allow any Christian in the congregation to miss such blessing by failing to challenge him to use his gifts for Christ, nor may he allow the body to suffer from the disuse of gifts that the sovereign Spirit thought necessary for the health and welfare of the entire body. All the gifts in a congregation are important and are needed by all (I Corinthians 12:14-31). As Peter says, it is a matter of stewardship:

As each one has received a gift, employ it in serving one another, *as good stewards* of the variegated grace of God (I Peter 4:10).

What is stewardship? It is the proper recognition and assumption of the duties that correspond to the abilities and opportunities that one has to perform them. From the other side of the picture: stewardship is simply being yourself; i.e., becoming all that God has given you the gifts to be. It is required of stewards that they be faithful (I Corinthians 4:2).

Training for Service

Training is an essential part of enlisting persons to use their gifts. Many persons fear to attempt what they could achieve because they know that they are not ready to do so, and they do not know how to get ready. Pastors must plan, enlist, and teach (and teach others to teach) every person who is asked to take on a new task. In ministry, training is of essence. The "discipling" of all nations (Matthew 28) speaks not merely of conversion, but goes far beyond that when it refers to keeping "all" that Christ commanded. Just as everywhere in the Scriptures, the new life of the believer is said to be both *taught* (by formal preaching, teaching, etc.) and also *caught* (by learning from models how to live and apply the teaching), so too one learns to serve Christ in *both* ways. Christ frequently instructed the disciples formally, but he also taught them by example. For a full discussion of this important matter, it might be well to consider again some of the scriptural data that I have brought together elsewhere.[12]

Paul frequently stressed the importance of modeling, or a good example

---

[12]What follows in the next few pages is an attempt to do just that.

in learning how to structure living. The importance of showing others how to obey God's commandments through example cannot be stressed too strongly. Role play or rehearsal may also be one valid means of extending the principle that scriptural discipline may be taught by example. Thus Paul called his readers not only to remember the words that he spoke, but also to recall the kind of life that he and his associates lived among them. Often principles can be impressed upon others most permanently and most vividly by means of example. Reference to example was not something unusual for Paul. Paul frequently used his own behavior as an example for others. This is apparent in passages like the fourth chapter of Philippians. There Paul directed his readers not only to pray and concentrate upon the things that were honorable, right, pure, lovely, and of good repute, but he continued:

> The things you have learned and received and heard and seen in me, practice these things: and the God of peace shall be with you (Philippians 4:9).

In the previous chapter of the same letter, he had already said,

> Brethren, join in following my example, and observe those who walk according to the pattern that you have in us (Philippians 3:17).

Paul considered his own life a model for new Christians. This emphasis is not limited to Philippians; Paul expressed the same thought in several other places. For instance, in I Corinthians 4:16 he wrote, "I exhort you therefore, be imitators of me."

Paul also mentioned modeling when he said, "You also became imitators" (I Thessalonians 1:6). The Greek term "imitator" is the same word from which the English word "mimic" comes. He wrote, "You became imitators of us and of the Lord." They learned, it seems, how to imitate the Lord by imitating what Paul was doing in imitation of his Lord. Again, Paul commended *them* for *becoming* models. After they learned how to imitate Paul in imitating the Lord, they themselves became examples for others; "You became an example to all the believers in Macedonia and Achaia" (I Thessalonians 1:7).

But it is not only Paul who stressed modeling. Peter similarly advised the elders of the church to which he was writing not only to "shepherd the flock of God," but without lording it over those allotted to their charge, to prove themselves to be "examples to the flock" (I Peter 5:3). The word used by Peter was *tupoi* ("types"). Elders are to be types or patterns for their flocks.

The idea of the model runs throughout the New Testament.[13]

This idea of modeling also occurs in John's writings, as well as in Peter's and Paul's. In III John 11, John's words show that he assumed that imitation will take place. He says, "Beloved, do not imitate what is evil, but what is good." He said, in effect:

> You're going to imitate. You can't help imitating. As a child you learned to imitate, and throughout life you are going to continue to imitate others. So make your imitation consciously purposeful by imitating that which is good.

The influence of older children in a home clearly demonstrates the importance of example. Younger children pick up their ways of speaking, their words, their actions and their attitudes. The influence of parents is even more striking. The influence which a counselor exerts in counseling is an important matter, as well. Counselors in all that they do, model, implicitly. At some times they model explicitly as well. And so the idea of modeling as a means of bringing about discipleship is something which must receive adequate attention.

Modeling was a principal teaching method of Jesus. At the beginning, it is of importance to notice that the Lord Jesus *appointed* the disciples as His students. The teacher sought out His pupils and accepted into His school only those whom He, Himself, had selected. Perhaps this principle of selectivity has too frequently been lost sight of, particularly in theological education. At their appointment, the purpose and methods that Jesus had in view, what He planned to do with these twelve disciples over the next few years and how He intended to do it, were explained. He appointed (or chose) twelve that they might be "with him." That is the key word; *"with him."* You may say, "I thought He was going to teach them; I thought He was going to *instruct them*." And isn't that what He did? Don't we see Jesus Christ subsequently sitting privately with His disciples explaining to them in detail what He taught the crowd in general? Do we not read of His instructing them in important truths? Don't we see Him teaching, teaching, teaching His disciples? Yes, we do. But teaching, as many people in modern times conceive of it, is thought of very narrowly. It is often considered to be merely that contact which takes place between a teacher and his students in which the teacher imparts factual information. Certainly, that is a large portion of teaching, and *nothing* I say here should

---

[13]Cf. I Thessalonians 1:6; Philippians 4:9; 3:17; I Corinthians 4:16; II Timothy 3:10; Thessalonians 3:9; I Timothy 4:12; Titus 2:7; Hebrews 13:7; I Thessalonians 1:7; III John 11 etc.

be construed to mean that I do not believe in the teaching of *content*. We *must* teach subject matter; indeed, much more than is taught elsewhere. But there is also much more to teaching than the teaching of content. That is why the Bible does not say that Jesus appointed twelve that He might *instruct* them. He does not say that He appointed twelve that He might send them to class. Nor does He say that He appointed twelve that they might crack the books and take His course. That was all a part of it, but, note, only a *part*. There is a much larger concept in these words: "He appointed twelve that they might be with Him." "With Him!" Think of all that meant. Those two words describe the fulness of Jesus' teaching. Such teaching is full; it is rounded, balanced and complete. For the length of His ministry, the disciples were to be with Him to learn not only what He taught them by word of mouth, but much more.

"How do you know?" you ask. "Aren't you possibly reading a lot into that phrase?" No, I don't think so, and I'll tell you why. The reason why I say that I'm not just reading my own ideas into this phrase is because in a definitive passage, Jesus Himself gave a description of teaching that accords exactly with this interpretation. In the sixth chapter of Luke, verse 40, He defines the pupil-teacher relationship, what goes on in that relationship and its results. Jesus says, "A pupil is not above his teacher, but everyone after he has been fully taught will be like his teacher." Now, did you get the full import of those words? He says, "Everyone" who is fully taught "will be like his teacher." Jesus did not say "will *think* like his teacher." That is part of it, but, again, it is only part of it. Jesus said that a pupil who has been properly (fully) taught "will *be* like his teacher." He will be like him, not just *think* like him. This passage helps us to understand the principles of education underlying Jesus' appointment of the twelve to be "with Him" in order to send them forth to teach. He was calling them to become His disciples (pupils) that they might be *with* Him in order to become *like* Him so that they might teach like Him.

"But, did these principles work? Did their education really make them 'like Him'?" The evidence provides a clear answer to that question. After Jesus had risen from the dead and ascended into heaven, He sent His Spirit back to continue His work through the Church. In Acts 4:13, Luke gives us a view of how the enemies of the Church looked upon the disciples (now called apostles) who were the leaders in this work:

> As they observed the confidence of Peter and John and understood that they were uneducated and untrained men (that is, formally so), they were marveling and began to recognize them as having been with Jesus.

The evidence is now complete. Look at it: He appointed twelve that they might be *with* Him. He said that a pupil, properly taught, will be like his teacher. And in the course of time others recognized that the disciples had become, in large measure, *like Him.*

Thus, in enlisting for evangelism, for teaching, for ushering, or for any number of other tasks in the church, it is important to provide discipleship (or apprenticeship) opportunities for instruction. Someone has said that in any organization, the key is persons; not systems. In one sense that is very true, but in another, it is dangerously deceptive. This is so because some systems, in emphasizing only content, delivered in formal contexts, tend to *keep persons away from persons.* The discipleship system in contrast *emphasizes* learning from the whole person. So persons are the key; but the system must allow for the personal element to surface meaningfully.

EXERCISE

For the Student

Using Romans 12:2-7 as a basis, develop a program for helping new Christians to discover their gifts.

For the Pastor

Determine how you best can help not only new converts, but also long standing members of your congregation to discover, develop and deploy their gifts.

CHAPTER ELEVEN
SETTING UP A PROGRAM

We shall turn at this time to a consideration of the church program. The pastor *leads,* through the dark valleys and the barren wastes to the green pastures and the still waters. But by what route? How does he help the members of his flock to walk in the paths of righteousness for the sake of God's Name? This he does by setting before himself and the flock three goals under one. To the honor of God, he seeks to achieve three, and only three purposes: (1) to lead the flock into the proper worship of the living God, (2) to lead the flock into edifying ways (i.e., the building up of itself in love, Ephesians 4:16), (3) to lead the flock into evangelistic outreaches. To accomplish these three goals the pastor must devise and follow a congregational blueprint, for it is only by a program, well planned and executed, that these ends may be attained. Jesus Christ followed a carefully laid out program in doing the will of God. It was a program planned and scheduled from "the foundation of the world."

Although the principle behind a biblical program is simple enough in concept, often it is difficult to apply. The principle is this: anything that does not enable the flock to worship God better, to be edified and to edify one another, and to evangelize the lost, must be eliminated; it has no place in the program of the church. On the other side of the page, however, is this: anything that would facilitate and foster these three biblical ends that is not already a part of the program, must be added as soon as possible. In short, any church program must honor God; and God is honored when His own revealed purposes are adopted and pursued.

A pastor, coming to a congregation, will bring new ideas about the ways and means of reaching these three scriptural goals. That, of course, is one value of a change of pastors. However, he must be careful not to expect everything in the pastorate to change, or to change right away. And, it is important for him to be ready to experience change himself. There are very few situations in which he will not learn from the new congregation, if he allows his own ideas and his own methods to be challenged.

He must be cautious about the way that he seeks to bring about change; otherwise he may become divisive. The only way to effect change solidly is by a thorough persuasion of the leadership of the congregation from the Word of God. Usually, this takes time. But if he is willing to work and wait, as a by-product he will learn patience, and when the change comes he will know that it is *solid* because it will be based upon conviction. Change by conviction is better than change by coercion. Every pastor must spend time winning the confidence of the leaders of the flock and of the members of the church by wise actions and teaching. During the period in which he is building confidence, he also should be making an analysis of the congregational situation. Using the three goals mentioned previously as his criteria, he should measure, compare and contrast every aspect of the current program. As a result, by the end of his first year, he ought to have a set of written objectives, listed in the order of priority, and built into a comprehensive five year plan.[1]

This five year plan should consist of general objectives and specific ways and means for reaching them. It should cover every aspect of congregational activity, stating what should be continued, what may be enhanced (and how), and what must be changed or eliminated. Hopefully, the period of building of confidence and the period of production of the plan will correspond roughly to one another, so that during the spring of the year (an ideal time; but any other will do), following his installation, he may begin to speak to the elders about his plan, and, hopefully too, may see the first stage of the new program develop and get under way during the fall that follows. (Fall, remember, is the *beginning* of the church year.)

The five year plan may be explained in part or in whole to the elders, as the pastor deems best at the time. Like Jesus, the pastor will find that he cannot unload everything upon others all at once because they are "not yet able to bear it." Often, more instruction, the encouragement from the success of the first phase of the five year plan, etc. will be needed before he can do so. Sometimes, the whole plan may be spelled out to the elders at once. The congregation, because it will contain people of every sort of spiritual growth ordinarily would be shown the plan in stages. But, at any rate, whether the entire plan is presented to the elders from the outset or only the first stage, it is essential that the *pastor himself* have the overall plan. Otherwise, what he does this year he may find it necessary to tear down the next. That is not to say that there can be no revisions. Certainly there can. Every pastor, like his people, should grow; growth (not to speak

---

[1]Cf. Appendix C for help in formulating a five year plan.

of God's own providential revisions) alters perspective. Yet, if there is no plan and no framework, all will be in flux and the pastor will not know where he is going. At all times, therefore, he should be operating toward something, not merely operating. He is a shepherd who ever seeks clearer waters and greener pastures for the flock. Leadership is always toward objectives. If he does not know what those objectives should be, how to attain them and persuade others to become enthusiastically committed to reaching them too, he can not be considered a *leader*. He himself will be like one of the sheep without a shepherd, wandering aimlessly.

A Covenantal Program

One basic principle for setting up a congregational program is to be sure that it is covenantal. That is to say, the pastor must be certain that the program in every way possible coordinates, rather than competes, with the family and home life of the members of the congregation. Far too often, the very meetings in which families are exhorted to preserve and develop deeper Christian values compete with the avowed purposes for which they were called. The calling of special meetings of the congregation must always be considered in respect to number (how many per month?), size (are crowds necessary; desirable?), content (is it truly additional to what can be given during the regular meetings?), time (flexibility? geared to family? could it be done on Sunday?) frequency (why not once per month rather than every week?) and persons invited (could the whole family come instead of a part only?). All special meetings should strengthen and encourage family life, not tend to tear it apart by placing demands upon it. Many things can be done *without* holding meetings. Decisions may be made by using the telephone, making conference calls or even using the mails (Why take six or eight men away from their families another night unless absolutely necessary?). And, why must the pastor exhort the congregation to turn out in crowds for weekday meetings? Our great concern for crowds often is sinfully motivated. Even when it is not, and there is a true desire to *help many,* the zeal is often "without knowledge." That is to say, on balance, the pastor would find that more good might be achieved by urging many of those who were inclined to come only out of a sense of duty to stay home instead. The persons who truly *need* to be at the meeting and *only* they are the ones who should attend. And, the pastor might *say so* when making the weekly announcements ("Now on Monday there is...Tuesday...Wednesday...Thursday...Friday...Saturday... and, of course, the regular services next Sunday. Please *do not attend* any of the meetings apart from the regular services of the church unless you have a good reason for doing so.[2] We want only those who especially need them to be present. Be sure to spend adequate time with your family this week, and you must see to it that church meetings do not keep you from doing so").

A Family Program

However, it is not *enough* to discourage running to meetings; at the same time the pastor must encourage a family program of worship, edification and evangelism. The need for this — all week long — has been felt by those who seek to provide it in urging attendance at a plethora of weekday meetings. Yet that solution is not viable, we have seen. But the need for more remains. That is why *a family program,* complementing the church program and coordinating with it should be developed. Instead of spending time at meetings away from the home, the pastor may encourage members of each family to spend time *in their homes, as families* in similar activities. These programs may be keyed into the regular services and meetings of the congregation. Rather than planning *meetings,* the pastor might more profitably plan and publish *materials* (family study, worship and activity guides) for weekday family use. The work accomplished may feed into the Sunday sermons (e.g., a guide for family Bible readings, complete with questions for study and discussion and outside reading materials, may be published each month in the congregational newsletter. Then Bible portions for each week may cover the passages upon which the sermon will be preached on the following Sunday evening. Ideas, suggestions, questions, examples, etc., may be phoned in to the church secretary or to a member appointed for that purpose by the Friday preceding the sermon. The pastor may then incorporate some of these in the message itself). Families may be encouraged to visit one another in order to foster Christian fellowship and hospitality. Participating members may have their family names drawn from a hat and published in the newsletter one month in advance ("The Harry Smiths will entertain the Wm. Joneses"). In this way families that otherwise might be reluctant to entertain one another will be encouraged to come to know each other better. There is no end to the possible ways and means for families to be encouraged to do things together.

Time and Planning

I have said a good bit already about time at an earlier point.[3] I wish to

---

[2]Five persons vitally involved are better than seventy five who are not. If too few attend, then perhaps the meeting is ill conceived.

[3]*Shepherding God's Flock,* Vol. I, "Repossessing time," Chapter VII, pp. 39-50.

make only one further observation: to get the time he needs, a pastor must *plan* for it. In the earlier discussion not only did I mention planning, but I provided basic worksheets for enabling the pastor to do so. Yet the discussion there focused more upon the pastor's individual planning. Here I wish to stress that all such planning must be fully coordinated with the corporate planning of the church. If the pastor does not consciously make every effort to coordinate his personal planning with congregational planning, continually he will find that his own plans will become subordinated to it.

That is to say that he must see to it that he always takes congregational planning into consideration when he makes personal plans. His datebook *cannot merely contain personal or even individual pastoral engagements;* it must also encompass all church activities which in any way bear upon his own time and scheduling.[4] Next, he must so insist upon the good stewardship of everyone's time that he influences the number as well as the date and time at which meetings are held. Rather than a matter of least significance, the pastor should work zealously at the question of setting the *proper* time and place for the next meeting of any group that he attends. Some organizations meet too frequently; he should say so, if he thinks that they could do with less meetings (if it is fellowship that is needed then that should be acknowledged and provided for in a better way). If the date means another day away from home, when a meeting could be held concurrently with the Church School or the Evening Youth Group, he should make that point. If the Women's Auxiliary could meet during the day, rather than spend another evening away from husbands and children, he may find it of importance to raise the question of the time of the meeting. In general, since time is so vital to him, the pastor should become increasingly alert to ways and means of saving time for himself and for others; he has none to waste.

One or two additional observations regarding time may be of help. It is of prime importance for every pastor to plan his work in such a way that he rarely ever does only one thing at a time. That is to say, whenever he puts out time and effort to do one thing, *if possible* he should be preparing (thereby) for several other things as well. For example, as he studies for a series of sermons, he decides to use some of the material developed in that preparation in an article that he has been asked to write for the

---

[4]Not that he has to attend all church meetings (as some pastors wrongly believe they should). The average conservative pastor probably could cut the number of meetings that he attends by at least half. Others, he could attend *less frequently*. At times, when forced to make the choice, he should wisely make appointments that overlap church meetings rather than those that overlap his family activities.

denominational magazine. At the same time, he determines to use some of it for a talk that he is scheduled to give at the Evangelical Ministerium next month. Continually, he insists (to himself *and to others*) that by this practice he will not allow himself to be spread too thinly. When he is requested to speak, *he* specifies the topic, and rarely allows others to do so for him, thereby allowing for time saving through overlap study and multifocused preparation.

Let me issue a warning about schedules. The schedule belongs to the pastor; he does not belong to it. He must make it, shape it, revise it. But, like a good friend, once he has it, he must stick to it (or revise it); he must *never ignore it*. Schedules must provide unscheduled cushion time for flexibility. This too is important.

Lastly, in all of his congregational planning, the pastor repeatedly should ask himself, "Is there someone else who could do this job?" and "Can someone else help me do this (or a part of it)?" Too few pastors know how to delegate. Those who have problems with learning to delegate, and who want to do something about it, might write out the two questions just mentioned on a card, place it on the desk (or under the glass on the desk) as a reminder to help them plan properly. But whatever they do, the key factor to keep in mind is that they will achieve the desired changes sooner and most dramatically if they combine delegation with planning. It is too difficult to delegate well *on impulse*. Delegation itself must be *planned* or (1) will not happen, or (2) should not happen in the shoddy way in which it has been handled.

EXERCISE

For the Student

Using a format similar to the one found in appendix C, draw up a five year plan for a congregation with which you are (or become) familiar. If you can secure the cooperation of the pastor of the congregation, work with him in the preparation of this program. Give him a copy and distribute a duplicate to each member of the class (include only the Program Planner and not the Worksheet).

For the Pastor

Using the Worksheet and Program Planner (appendix C), draw up a five year program for your church. Take your time, and write in pencil so that changes may be made later. But set yourself a deadline of no less than one month for setting up the objectives of the five year program of change.

CHAPTER TWELVE
ORGANIZATIONS IN THE CONGREGATION

It is vital for the pastor (and through him for everyone in the congregation) to understand that all of the activities of a congregation, including those carried on by organizations like the Youth Groups, the Church School, the Women's Society and the Choir are *a part of the congregational program*.[1] These organizations are not separate entities answerable only to God and themselves, but a portion of the congregational effort subject to the oversight and discipline of the elders of the congregation. Often this fact is neither known nor is the proper relationship of such organizations to the board of elders a reality.

The fact must be communicated and the reality must come into being. Otherwise, as the result of independent attitudes and practices foreign to the New Testament, growing disunity, conflict, inability to check heresy, inefficiency and ineffectiveness will result, all to the dishonor of God and the destruction of the flock.

More often than not, the difficulties in a congregation grow out of the failure to conform to biblical principles of church government. In the Scriptures, it is a plurality of elders to whom is given the rule in a congregation; all that happens is subject to their approval and oversight. If there is no one central, coordinating center of authority in the congregation, no shepherdly leadership, the flock will be scattered. Members will begin to wander off. Factions will grow and the flock will be divided. Remember, flocking is a significant task of shepherdly leadership; sheep do not flock *on their own*. Shepherdly leadership helps each organization to see itself as *a part of the whole,* not as a separate entity.[2]

---

[1] On no other basis can such organizations be justified biblically. This justification rests upon viewing organizations as congregational ways and means developed for carrying out Christ's mandates for worship, edification and evangelism.

[2] It is important for the various organizations to communicate with each other. Rarely is this done. Leaders in each group should meet at least quarterly (in addition to one yearly joint planning session in the spring) to discuss matters of cooperation, coordination and united efforts. Otherwise, organizations will find themselves working *against* one another and the family. The pastor and other elders should attend these joint sessions (perhaps held on Sunday evenings at the time of the Youth Meeting).

How can such a unified system be taught and effectuated? There is only one sure way: *authority is demonstrated when the responsibility that accompanies it is assumed.* Nothing can cause more difficulty than for a pastor or his elders to begin to assert their authority, rightful as it may be, by issuing directives and leveling criticisms *without shouldering the burdens of authority* that are involved in oversight.

What are those burdens? Well, responsibilities differ from organization to organization, but such questions as showing interest in and acquaintance with the organization and its members, helping out as a trouble shooter when there are problems and difficulties, sharing in the decisions made at business meetings, expressions of appreciation for accomplishments, willingness to attend meetings, prompt, fair responses from the elders to questions or suggestions stemming from the organization, and regular prayerful concern for the projects it undertakes are fundamental. When pastors, themselves, take the lead in such matters they are in a position to encourage their elders to do so too.

It is possible, of course, for designated elders to exercise special oversight toward particular congregational organizations. This is often a good way to assure responsible concern and rule. When such a plan is adopted, it is wise to have reports on each organization from its overseeing elder at every regular elders meeting.[3] This keeps the need for oversight constantly before the board of elders and lays the responsibility of concern for at least one organization heavily upon each elder. If he continually reports "no report," the board (or perhaps first the pastor quietly behind the scenes) asks: "Is there some reason why you are unable to give adequate oversight to this organization, John? Is there anything we can do to help?" His answer may lead to the discovery of difficulties in John's life (disorganization, overloaded schedule, priority problems, growing lack of interest, laziness) or perhaps in the organization itself ("They keep changing the dates of their business meetings" or "They told me that they didn't want the elders shoving their oars in" or "Really, there's nothing to report; nothing significant ever happens").

Let us consider a couple of typical problem areas in two specific organizations to discover concretely how problems may be prevented or remedied by proper oversight. We shall take a look first at the Choir, then at the Church School.

The Choir

To begin with, several issues seem to be perennial Choir problems. Since

---

[3]Probably held on a monthly basis.

they are, there is every reason to take steps *beforehand* to avoid the difficulties.[4] Good oversight is first preventive. Here are three such problems: (1) Who may become members of the Choir? Believers only? Church members only? Trained singers only? (2) Who determines the type of hymns sung? Is the emphasis to be placed upon words or upon music? (3) How can the Choir be deactivated as a gossip network that so often crackles with information (and *mis*information)?

Proper oversight will require that each organization of the congregation shall have a set of by-laws drawn up and approved by the session in consultation with the leadership of that organization. These should be duplicated and made available to all who are involved. These by-laws will contain such information as (for the Church School) qualifications for teachers or (for the Choir) qualifications for membership. All by-laws will state prominently that the organization is an extension of the congregation, holds to its particular objectives, and what its place and functions are in relationship to the whole. Its relationship to the elders should be made crystal clear. Obviously the by-laws themselves when properly constructed and used, will help to keep problems such as (1) and (2) from arising. The by-laws are preventive and must attempt to *anticipate* as many difficulties as possible.

But by-laws, good and useful as they may be, cannot do everything. Indeed, they are only as useful as the *persons* who operate within them. And, moreover, it is only the right *persons* who finally can deal with such problems as (3), the gossip network. It is important, then, not only for the board of elders to exercise keen oversight toward the Choir, but also for them to select the choir director with great care. It is essential, for instance, to find a person of sound Christian conviction who (1) will be concerned not only about the quality of the music, but also about the quality of its message, (2) will be able to work with people and who (3) will be able to set the proper tone for each choir practice by explaining the import of the message of the music and its purpose in the service, and who (4) will be alert to and able to deal with such matters as gossip when he sees them arise.[5]

Usually the pastor will find it necessary to draw up sample by-laws

---

[4] Always a good policy; much better than the usual policy of doing nothing until something tragic happens.

[5] Sometimes it is better to have no choir than to have one that is poorly directed (and by directed I mean ability to direct in all four of the above areas). If choices must be made, it is probably more important to sacrifice first-rate music for the other qualities. It is not wrong to pay a choir director, but better still is to discern gifted persons and appoint them to the directorship and to membership in the choir. Sometimes it is better to pay to send a trusted member of the congregation to school for further instruction in directing than to hire someone

himself (or at least one such) in order to present the matter to the board of elders. The pastor may have to show them how the by-laws are designed to prevent problems from developing. When introducing these to the organization in question, he must do the same for the members, but only after already having taken the time to explain these facts to the leadership of the organization and after enlisting their help (indeed, if the Choir leader or Sunday School superintendent himself can enthusiastically and clearly give the explanation, so much the better).[6]

The Church School

Let us now take up a typical Church School problem (one that we have considered already, the qualification of teachers). We saw how by-laws can help to forestall difficulties in this area. But in what ways can persons having the qualifications set forth in those by-laws be found? Surely, they do not usually walk in the church door, fully prepared, and announce their availability. Usually, these persons must be discovered, appointed, trained and provided with adequate resources. One way to provide training is in a yearly Teacher Training Course for prospective and appointed teachers. The course may be taught by the pastor in conjunction with the revolving Adult Church School Curriculum at the tertiary level during one of the four quarters.[7] But a teacher training course, devoted to the general principles of teaching is not, in itself, adequate. Instead there must be an apprenticeship or discipling program available too. It is even possible for the pastor to develop a teacher or two to teach the Teacher Training Course also. In doing so he would use the same basic apprenticeship model that he uses in training men to teach the other courses in the curriculum. That is to say, the first time through, the pastor himself teaches the course, developing a syllabus, assignments, lectures, etc. He then appoints someone who sat in on the course and who, by his participation gives evidence of understanding and gifts to do so, to teach it the next time, while the pastor sits in (behind the scenes, the pastor coaches, gives helpful criticism, encourages, trouble shoots and, in general, gives strong backing). Thereafter, the teacher teaches the course by himself. Since it is a teacher training course, in most instances the pastor would be wise to select

---

from outside the body. Volunteer directors, and volunteer choirs bring problems. Oversight involves work by the pastor and elders in discovering, developing and deploying the gifts God has provided within the body.

[6]Remember, if the pastor and/or elders drew up the by-laws *in conjunction with* the organization's leadership (as suggested above) support and fuller understanding is more likely to be obtained from the leadership.

[7]See the next chapter for a description of this program and an explanation of these terms.

someone ahead of time to sit in for this purpose, someone who already has demonstrated ability to teach.

So, just as it is not enough to adopt by-laws for governing the Choir (we have seen that proper leadership is also required), so too it is not sufficient merely to set forth by-laws for a Church School (determining among other things the qualifications for teachers). In addition, various ways and means for discovering persons with adequate gifts and for developing those gifts also must be worked out. Most failures in attaining well thought through, doctrinally sound results come from two omissions: (1) failure to secure the proper persons by appointment; (2) failure to train them by both formal and apprenticeship methods. What has been said here about the Church School, and earlier about the Choir, holds for every other organization as well, simply because organizations are organizations of *people*. People have different capabilities, maturity of doctrine and life, concerns and commitments. The personal factor, in the end, often is what really makes the difference.

But while this is true, let us not forget that the right person, *without* adequate training, with an inadequate task description, with no authority or without the proper resources cannot be expected to do the job either. The pastor, for instance, may not sit back with a sigh of relief, thinking that all will be well now that the church has hired a theological seminary student to work with the youth. That student may or may not be the right one to work with youth. He may or may not need much instruction. All of these matters must be considered and the pastor or some elder alerted by him to do so must stand closely by to be sure that the work is done properly. The Youth worker may need heavy backing at first to help him see needs and even to decide how best to meet them. If he becomes so bogged down with his studies that the youth work suffers, he may need encouragement and help in drawing up a personal priority list leading to a new and more realistic study/work schedule. Usually we forget that able people with strong convictions often need help too.

Appreciation

And, in speaking of getting the best service of God from those who work in the church, the pastor (and he by example and suggestion should teach others to do so too) should take a leaf from the Chief Shepherd's notebook. He must learn to express appreciation for work well done ("well done, you good and faithful servant" is what Christ will say). Even in some of those seven Churches where there was little to approve, Jesus (nevertheless) found something that He honestly could commend ("this you have") and stated that first. Appreciation is an oil that it is essential for him to apply freely if the pastor wishes to keep the complex machinery of congregational activity running smoothly.[8]

EXERCISE

For the Student or the Pastor

In the space below jot down elements you would like to have in a set of by-laws for the Choir. Students, in groups of four or five then should together draw up an actual set of by-laws. A pastor, in conjunction with some neighboring pastors, may do the same.

---

[8]For further examples of the expression of appreciation, study the New Testament epistles (especially those by Paul). Begin with a study of Romans 16.

CHAPTER THIRTEEN
A CHURCH SCHOOL FOR ADULTS

The Adult Department of the Church School, apart from those exceptional situations in which the presence of an unusual teacher has made the difference, has a dissatisfying record of mediocrity. The sad level of half-hearted participation and performance, so frequently exhibited in such classes, usually parallels rather closely a low level of weekday Christian living that is part and parcel of the same failure. This failure stems largely from an inability to study and apply the Scriptures practically and in depth.[1] Existing programs, for the most part, fail to satisfy this need. As a consequence, neither businessmen nor housewives know how to get the help that they need from the Scriptures when they need it — when they have decisions to make and problems to solve on Thursday and Saturday. If this need to enable Christians to use their Bibles more effectively and practically is to be met, *adults must be taught how to do so.*

Retracing the missionary journeys of Paul for the umpteenth time in their Sunday School careers, useful and important as that may be for its purpose, will not meet that need. Something far more ambitious, far more comprehensive, far more well-rounded must be done. The proposal in this section, successfully followed in various forms in three congregations, endeavors to point the way (many modifications and improvements are necessary) to a solution to the problem.

To begin with, consider the odds against which the average Church School[2] teacher labors:

[1] I am convinced that while there are a great number of exceptions to this rule, the lethargy in the church, and the low level of living evidenced, derives more frequently than we may realize from ineptness than from lack of desire. Of course, the two are not mutually exclusive: failure to achieve often leads to resignation, which (in turn) may lead to lethargy. Discussions with hundreds of laymen concerning this matter, however, lead to the conclusion that great changes for good could be effected quickly by introducing a plan of teaching that would overcome the difficulties I have mentioned. That is why this program was envisioned and is articulated here.

[2] I prefer not to use the title "Sunday School" because of the unfortunate connotations that this word has for so many adults. To each of them it may mean many things, but rarely do the words convey the idea of a genuine school where significant learning takes place. Pastors would be wise when introducing the new plan to give the school a different title.

1. Usually he has had no training in teaching.
2. He has had no special training in his subject matter.
3. His class labors under no stated obligation to learn.
4. He has no feedback (examinations, reports, papers, etc.) to help him determine whether what he attempts to teach is in fact being learned.
5. He must work in truly abysmal learning conditions.
   a. There are no desks, no textbooks, etc.
   b. There is no homework required.
   c. No one is expected to take notes.
   d. Classes meet only every seventh day.
   e. Levels of understanding are ignored.
6. He must teach new material each week, never repeating material taught before.
7. He must become a generalist, equally able to teach Old Testament or New Testament, Bible geography, or Doctrine or anything else.
8. He teaches in an open-ended context — on and on — with no semesters or other terms (etc.) marked out.
9. He has no "time off."
10. He has no opportunity to learn and grow under another's teaching since all teaching is coterminous.

These considerations are only a few of the more obvious ones that might be mentioned. Clearly, pastors ought to be concerned about them. If, as shepherds, their task is to equip the saints for their works of ministry, pastors must make every effort to sharpen this dull but important tool. Millions of members waste countless hours of time every year in adult classes, that could be thoroughly productive.

The average Adult Church School either ought to be abandoned or revitalized; it should not be permitted to go on as it has. The lives of many persons are affected adversely because they think that the mediocrity that they experience is the best that Christianity has to offer. It is not, and pastors must not allow them to think so. The Adult School, instead, can be turned into a challenging and exciting learning experience.

"I'm willing to try almost anything," you may respond. "I know what you're talking about!" Fine, if you are willing to work at making the school in your church a genuine *school,* capable of *teaching* and thus influencing the lives of many adults positively for Jesus Christ, I assure you that it can be done. But, let me warn you, not only will you run into resistance from various quarters, you also will discover that the transformation will call for work on your part. You must be ready and able to devote yourself to the task for a period of time to get it under way. If you are game, read on. If not, skip the rest of this section of the book, and turn again to it only after you have spent another month observing the futility of what so often is labeled (wrongly) "teaching" in the adult class(es).

If you are prepared to go ahead (out of eagerness, despair or both), let us begin by asking the question: What are the prime goals of the church? The answer is amply supplied by what is called The Great Commission (Matthew 28:19,20). The passage should not be allocated solely to missionaries; it is *your* overall directive for church life and activity. After all, when you think about it, you *and* your congregation are converts on a foreign mission field. Jerusalem was the home base; you live in one of the "uttermost parts" of the world (cf. Acts 1:8).

The so-called Great Commission describes the church and her work in *educational* terms. Her task is to "make disciples"; that is, to gather in *students* (as the word disciple means). Every Christian is a student, who when he becomes a part of Christ's church (thereby) becomes a student of Christ in Christ's school (the church). The call to baptism is a call to matriculation and to admission into the institution. But *once* they become a part of the church (the school), they are to be *taught* (v. 20). Adults, therefore, should be encouraged to learn, should understand that learning is a large part of what their membership and participation in church life is all about, and should be given genuine opportunities to learn not only in preaching contexts but also in the Church School

The teaching that is in view (v. 20) is not casual or limited to certain areas, but both extensive and intensive. It is to extend to the whole corpus of information and skills that were given to the church by Christ: "*all* that I commanded." And, notice especially, it does not extend merely to the acquisition of information, but *beyond,* to the application of truth to life ("teaching to *observe*"). Thus the teaching must be so intensive that it aims at influencing life, and is conducted in such a way that, in truth, it does bring about such changes as were commanded by Jesus.

Now, of course, that is a large order. Yet, it is what Christ requires, and it accords exactly with the task of the pastor-teacher in Ephesians 4:11,12 Your efforts are to build up your sheep by *teaching* them to *observe* all that Christ commanded so that they may serve Him well in ministry through the use of their gifts.[3] The time and effort, therefore, that you expend in effort

---

[3]The task-oriented titles "pastor" and "teacher" correspond nicely to the two tasks *teaching* (teacher) to *observe* (pastor).

to improve the teaching program in your congregation, is well spent.[4] You must see that it is at the heart of your responsibility and not simply ancillary to it.

Let us then take those three factors mentioned earlier and examine them more fully. Jesus requires:

1. *Complete, comprehensive teaching:* "teach them to observe *all* things that I commanded" (what Paul called the "whole counsel of God" — Acts 20:27, 20).
2. *Effective teaching:* "teach them to *observe* all things that I commanded."
3. *Correct teaching:* "teach them to observe all *things that I commanded.*"

It is those three elements that continually must guide the pastor as he sets up and evaluates any program of teaching in the church. They too are the criteria by which he may test the present teaching program. He may (must) ask such questions as "How much of the body of Christian truth is being taught?," "How clearly is this truth being made known?," "How well are the lives of those taught being affected by it?," and "How accurately is it being presented?" Whatever in a program that hinders students from receiving comprehensive and accurate teaching that edifies must be eliminated; whatever enables it must be added.

Let us ask, "Can the average layman learn more, considerably more than he usually does?" The answer is yes. Not only has Jesus required *all* of the students in his school to learn *all* that he commands, but there are institutions that have demonstrated that when the effort to do so is made, man-in-the pew Christians can be taught great amounts of truth effectively and in ways that influence their lives significantly. Take, for instance, the work of the Bible School movement. I refer not only to the day schools but to the night school programs carried on in many cities throughout the country. Far more teaching is offered there than is usually taught in the average Church School. But why is this so? Does it need to be? Why must members of your congregation take out another night away from their families and spend extra funds to get from some other source what your church failed to teach? Moreover, can you be sure that what is taught there altogether accurate? Will not the doctrine often be of a least-common-denominator variety since persons from such a variety of backgrounds must be served? Will not many important biblical truths therefore, be bypassed or distorted? Could you not develop a better program in your

---

[4]Well spent because it is spent doing what the Lord commands.

congregation, one that retains all of the strengths of the Bible School (which only a limited number of your adults would/could attend anyway) but eliminates all of its weaknesses? Yes, you could!

How? Well, having convinced your elders (and that may mean such things as at first running an experimental pilot program for a part of the adult members who agree to participate), you must then carve out the time for such a program. That will be your first real hurdle. You cannot either teach or learn when you do not have sufficient time to do the job well. The half hour teaching time that some adult classes allot to themselves is not only insufficient, it is preposterous. Who can learn anything worthwhile in a half hour, one-day-per-week setting? Do not try to make the change, therefore, unless you can allocate sufficient time in which to effect it. Otherwise, your efforts will be set for failure before you have begun.

One way to recapture valuable time is to eliminate the "worship service" or the "opening exercises" or other preliminaries that usually take up to half of the time devoted to the Church School. The adults do not need this anyway. Anyone who is old enough to worship in the regular worship service will find this duplication unnecessary and time consuming. Worship at home and in the regular worship services of the congregation is sufficient if carried out well. By dropping this opening period, and beginning to teach immediately after prayer, a full hour for teaching can be obtained.

Yet, a better arrangement is possible. If the Church School can begin at 9:30 A.M. instead of 10:00 A.M., that additional half hour provides for much more opportunity to do *many more* things. Look at some of the possibilities:

1. There can be two teaching periods each Sunday:
     9:30 - 10:10 (40 minutes)
     10:15 - 10:55 (40 minutes)[5]
2. Two periods each morning allow for opportunity for teacher (adult and otherwise) to sit in on one of these so that they too may receive instruction.
3. Two periods allow for other Bible related courses, such as those taught in Bible Schools, to be offered *along with* (instead of *replacing*) regular courses in the direct study of the Bible. Courses in cults, evangelism, Bible Geography, etc. can be taught.
4. Opportunities to do more significant things in the children's and youth departments are opened up.

[5]Forty minute periods are not as adequate as single hour-long periods, but they are quite sufficient when doubling up on periods. The five minute breaks at 10:10 and 10:55 allow for time to change classes and to get to morning worship (11:00).

5. Other special courses (teacher training, new converts courses, etc.) may be offered at one of the two hours without replacing a Bible Study course and rather than taking time during the week to do so.
6. The change of teachers and subjects that two periods allow is refreshing, especially if one of the two teachers is not too apt.

These suggestions are only a few of the many possibilities that the two period system provides. The flexibility it builds into the program is what both pastors and members alike will find most desirable.

The next concept to visualize is the need to break down the Sunday School *class* concept in favor of the *course* concept. The *class* is a group of persons of varying levels of spiritual maturity and understanding who are trying to learn together. Frequently visitors and unbelievers also appear in such classes. This does not provide for optimum learning conditions. The idea that you will destroy the fellowship of the class is fallacious. If the Church School exists primarily for fellowship, then let us acknowledge this openly and call it the *fellowship* hour. Then, in all honesty, the period can be designed to promote fellowship (I am not saying that this could not be done, nor that it should not be done periodically, say, once every two months). There are many other better ways to promote fellowship (not that learning together will not do so too). But, if the primary purpose of the Church School is to promote learning, then that purpose must not be sacrificed for a secondary one.

The course concept develops from and, indeed, is suggested by the idea of complete or comprehensive teaching ("teach them to observe *all things*"). There is much to learn, and it is not all the same. Therefore, in order to teach more systematically and thoroughly, and in order to be sure that the full range of biblical concern is covered, a curriculum consisting of various courses to be pursued over a period of time should be developed. Of course, no curriculum will be perfect or complete, but without one, teaching becomes hit-or-miss.

The courses may be developed as 10 or 12 week periods offered on a quarter system (with Fall, Winter, Spring and Summer quarters). If courses are 12 weeks in length, they will require 48 of the 52 weeks in the year. That permits the Church School to have four *special* programs each year (Christmas, Easter, Rally Day?, Reformation Day?). If the 10 week concept is adopted, more flexibility is built in: (1) More special programs are possible, (2) Field trip days can be developed, (3) Fellowship hours can be inserted periodically, etc.

The concept of courses allows individual teachers to specialize; the idea of a curriculum allows them to teach courses again and again, thus becoming more proficient in doing so. Courses *build* over the years as one teaches them over again. The most experienced college professor would refuse to teach only new material, on any and all subjects, to a motley group of students, yet we expect inexperienced and untrained teachers to do just that! Teachers (especially if there is a large Church School) may belong to departments (Bible, Doctrine, Christian Living, Bible History and Geography, etc.) These departments may wish to plan their offerings together with the aid and direction of the pastor.

The concept of courses allows a teacher to think of his teaching more systematically, in terms of 10-12 week packages, rather than in an open ended who-knows-when-we'll-change-or-stop manner. And, if he is allowed to teach no more than one course per half year, and only every other quarter (2 courses per year), this means that (1) he can at each Sunday sit in on a class taught by someone else (he can learn about methodology in teaching thereby as well as benefit from the instruction[6]); (2) he can have two one-quarter breaks during which he can prepare ahead of time for his next quarter's course. While not every Church School will have enough teaching personnel at the outset to effect this, it should be an aim. Since the curriculum envisions offering a teacher training unit, the possibility of developing teachers is good. Since this sort of instruction *builds* members more quickly, teaching potential is realized more rapidly than one may realize.

Now, let us look at curriculum possibilities. I have suggested a basic division between the two periods:

> Periods One (9:30 - 10:10) Bible Related Courses
> Period Two (10:15 - 10:55) Bible Study Courses

Bible-related courses focus on Bible study too, but they are not designed as direct Bible Study courses. Hence, the distinction. A one-year sample curriculum may look something like this:

---

[6]Too many teachers dry up from failure to participate in a course themselves. It is not good always to give and never to receive.

1976

		FALL	WINTER	SPRING	SUMMER
Level I	Period One	Bible Doctrine #1 (Scripture)	Bible Interpretation	Bible Doctrine #2 (God)	Personal Evangelism
	Period Two	N. T. Introduction	Bible #1 (John)	Bible #2 (Judges)	Bible #3 (Acts)
Level II	Period One	Christian Living in the Home	Bible Doctrine #3 (sin/salvation)	Christian Living at Work	Cults
	Period Two	O. T. Introduction	Bible #4 (Romans)	Bible #5 (Proberbs)	Bible #6 (1 Corinthians)
Specials	Period One	Teacher Training		Prospective Elders' Course	
	Period Two	New Converts Course			

The pattern above does not necessarily represent what you and your congregation would do. But it does visualize the possibilities. According to this sample, in the fall at the 9:30 hour (Period One) three courses would be taught to three different groups of people. Those taking Bible Doctrine #1, the Doctrine of Scripture, would be starting out on the first year of the curriculum (designated as Level I). Those taking the Christian Living in the Home course would have already taken the eight Level I courses offered during the year 1975. Those taking Teacher Training are a special group who wish to teach, but who need preparation in order to do so. Presumably, the sample would represent a program that has been in operation for only two years. Several more levels are possible (up to as many as you want, though probably not more than VI or VII in all). Some of the titles of additional courses that might be offered are:

Period One Courses	Period Two Courses	Specials
Bible Doctrine #4 (Sanctification)	Bible # (any number of Bible books may be studied)	Greek Visitors' Class
Bible Doctrine #5 (Church)	Life & Work of Christ	Teacher's Training
Bible Doctrine #6 (Future)	The Parables The Miracles Prophecy	
Christian Living in the Community	etc.	
Church History		
Defense of the Faith		
Bible Geography, Manners & Customs		
Bible Archeology		
Cults		
Personal Evangelism		

Naturally, you may add, subtract or alter this program in any number of ways. It is designed for maximum flexibility. I have used it in small congregations and large, with few initial teachers and courses, and with many.

Resources

One more matter must be mentioned before closing this chapter. There should be a true teaching situation. Chairs should not be positioned in a circle, but should be purchased with an arm writing tablet, or should be placed at tables or desks. Note-taking should be encouraged. Loose leaf notebooks may be purchased by the Church School with dividers labeled to correspond to the various courses offered. Not only notes, but coordinated course-outlines, handouts, syllabi, workbooks, etc., could be kept in the binder.

Adequate visual aids should be purchased — overhead projectors, chalk boards, maps, pictures, etc. A cassette videotape recorder might be utilized with great profit since lectures for some courses could be prerecorded for use at later points. (This could save on personnel.) The cost today is no longer prohibitive.

Students in the courses should be given homework, should do research, give reports and take examinations (which they may grade themselves).

Textbooks (and syllabi developed by teachers or by the pastor) are valuable assets. These materials begin to build personal libraries for Christian families. Moreover, with a program like this, a good church library is an essential (and it will be *used*).

All-in-all, the concerned pastor will discover (I think) that this suggested approach will point toward the solution to some of the most serious problems of stimulating interest and personal growth that he may be pondering. Much prayerful time and effort has been expended in developing and effectuating this program. It is not untried! It works. One 80-year old woman told me that after one year in this program she had learned more from Sunday School than in the 75 or so years previous. While not everyone responds in the same fashion, the overall response has always been similar. Teachers especially profit from it. And they begin to enjoy their teaching in a new way. Many soon develop a new competence and a new ability to teach. Persons qualified for the eldership emerge more rapidly, and in general the whole church is affected for good. Try it, but not half-heartedly. Either determine to throw your fullest effort into it or wait until you are ready to do so. It cannot be undertaken successfully unless you do.

CHAPTER FOURTEEN
LEADING CHILDREN AND YOUTH

The pastor, as a good shepherd, cares not only for the sheep, but also for the lambs. God, as Shepherd, describes His concern for those little ones in the flock in these tender terms:

> Like a shepherd He will tend His flock. In His arms He will gather the lambs, And carry them in His bosom;

He will gently lead the nursing ewes (Isaiah 40:11). Surely, the risen Savior's reinstatement of Peter also placed a strong emphasis upon pastoral ministry to children when he commanded: "Tend my lambs" (John 21:15).

Pastors today can do no less. Their concern for the youth of the congregation must in every way exemplify and be guided by the Lord's own deep concern.

While it is not possible to develop a program for the leadership and pastoral care of children and youth in this volume (perhaps something fuller can be done at a later point in another volume devoted solely to this subject), I do wish to say at least something to pastors about each of these areas of pastoral leadership that may prove of significance to them and through them to their congregations by arousing them to take action. Because of their place of leadership, pastors are able to exercise great influence upon the work carried on with children and youth. There are a few large concerns that I wish to share, therefore, for whatever benefit they may have in stirring the thinking of pastors who lead.

Junior Church — A Live Option?

There are two diametrically opposed viewpoints among conservative Bible believing pastors (and their people) about the place of the child in the worship service. Should all of the children once they are able to waddle from the nursery be lined up for an hour (or hours) on the pew alongside of their parents? Does this demonstrate the covenant relationship of God to the family, and does it train children in the ways of worship for a lifetime to come? Or, as others aver does it rather train them to sleep in church, to endure a sermon that they cannot understand, and thereby teach them how not to hear it? Does this train them not to worship at all, but to fiddle around with hymn books, bulletins, etc.?

Clearly the prejudicial wording of the sentences in the previous paragraph makes it abundantly plain that I adhere to the second position. While surely children should appear on the pews as early as it is possible for them to participate meaningfully in the morning worship service, I do not think that it does them or anyone else (neither parents nor others nearby can worship well with the interruptions they cause) any good to be hauled into place every Sunday for an hour's worth of who knows what. Anything but optimal learning/worshipping conditions exist. But, what does the Bible say about this? Well, the answer to that question is: "Nothing directly." But there is a principle that is articulated in the Book of Nehemiah that does carry great significance; this principle is set forth in Chapter 8, verses 2 and 3:

> Then Ezra the priest brought the law before the assembly of men, women and *all who could listen with understanding....* And he read ... in the presence of men and women and *those who could understand;* and all the people were attentive to the book of the law.

Here, the children who were too young to understand the public reading, and explanation of the Scriptures (cf. also vv. 8,9), were excluded from the assembly. This did not break the covenant unity of the family. Rather than to show this unity artificially, there was a deeper concern expressed: to assure the attentive listening of those who were present. The purpose of worship is not to demonstrate the unity of the family. Those who assembled as a result neither were disturbed by the restlessness of the children, nor were the children disturbed by the restrictions placed upon them to sit and stand quietly during a meeting in which they could not participate meaningfully. Thus, this wise measure was taken to assure the attentiveness of all assembled. That this particular meeting was longer in duration than the average worship service is granted, but notice that the text says nothing about the exclusion of the children because of the time factor. Rather, the operative factor was simply their *inability to understand.*[1] That factor seems to be the determinative one, therefore, in deciding (1) whether

---

[1]Since the meeting was of extraordinary length, one would expect that this fact would be stressed if it was the determinative one. That it is never coupled with the exclusion of the children, clearly shows that it was not the significant factor involved in that decision.

children should be admitted to the church service, and (2) when any particular child should be. Note too that no specific age level was mentioned. Understanding of the reading and of the preaching of the Scriptures, therefore, is the only element involved in the decision to admit or exclude. Since young children differ so radically in their readiness, they would not all be able to move into the adult worship service at the same age. Parental judgment, or possibly some simple tests of the ability to understand might determine when that time would come for any given child.

The concept of "Junior Church" is one way to go. However, I hold no brief for that particular name. Perhaps a term that more clearly indicates the preparatory nature of the period would be preferable. I have no desire to nail down one title over another, so I will not even venture a suggestion; it is the content of the period that is of significance. During this time there is an ideal opportunity for the assistant pastor, a seminary intern, elders in rotation, deacons, or others from the congregation who have the competence to do so, to give instruction about the elements of worship that make up the adult worship service from which the children have been excluded. This instruction, of course, will be on their level, with variety conforming to the attention span of the children (including lots of singing), and with at least minimal participation on their part (taking up the collection, etc.). The Lord's prayer and the apostle's creed can be explained. The place and use of the offering may be discussed. The purpose of singing and preaching may be explored. Information on such simple matters as how to use a bulletin or such crucial ones as how to listen to a sermon may be given. Sometimes, when there is to be a baptism, when the Lord's supper is celebrated, when new members are admitted, or when elders or deacons are to be ordained, the children may be instructed about these features of the service in their own meeting and then (either prior to or after that instruction, according to the order of the event in the order of worship) they may visit the worship service during the specific time when that event occurs. There should be plenty of opportunity for the children to ask questions and to make observations about what they see. When children have been thoroughly instructed about what is going on in the other worship service, while also conducting worship on their own level they will begin their attendance at the regular services with much more understanding and at an age where they can enter into the worship in a meaningful way. And you will find that they look forward with anticipation rather than boredom to becoming participants in the worship service. Moreover, rather than having to relearn better habits of worship after having learned bad ones for so long (some adults have never unlearned the bad patterns that they developed as children!), they are more likely to start out on a better footing. This will be so not only because of prior instruction, but also (and, remember, this is the *prime* emphasis of Nehemiah) because of their greater maturity.

The church that does not provide some such help for its younger children will regret it. Pastors may find it necessary to exercise courageous leadership in introducing a program of this type, since there are many laymen who (out of pride, or quite sincerely) will object. Yet the biblical principle must prevail. And for the sake of the church — both adults who wish to worship with less interference, but especially for the sake of the children who are learning all the wrong things on the pews — the pastor must take the initiative and fly straight through the flack.

Work With Youth

While it is not desirable to mix Junior Highs and Senior Highs, it is essential to view them together in planning and in coordinating the Youth Work in the church. To think of their several programs in airtight compartments is a serious error. Because so often we have done so, in many ways we create problems that emerge in working with High School Youth Groups. Yet we fail to realize that these problems are of our own making. Pastors must come to see that the Senior High product is manufactured in the Junior High period, and that if it does not suit our standards at a later point, that is because too little early concern was given about the kind of product that we wished. The *key* to building a good Senior High Work is to mold it when it is still in Junior High. Junior Highs are plastic; many of the ways of Senior Highs (more often than not) already are set. While God can surely change Senior Highs, (often in spectacular ways) it is unwise to wait till then to ask Him to do so. Especially can we see that this is so when we realize that we are responsible for not having done more at the earlier period.

The Junior-Senior High programs should be viewed as two parts of a whole. Each segment bears a meaningful relation to the other. In the Junior High period the product is *manufactured* for *use* in the Senior High period. If a faulty product is handed down, then it becomes difficult to make the proper use of the energy and power of the High Schoolers. Indeed, precisely what we find is that their strength often is used destructively. I am firmly convinced that the secret to a significant youth work, therefore, is found in the successful pursuit of such a sequential pattern. The Junior High work should (self-consciously) be aimed at *preparing* these students for what they will be doing as Seniors in the church.

But, what should Seniors do? Many things, concretely speaking, might be mentioned. But, more generally (I suggest), they should be *using* their faith. Individually and corporately, within and without, they should be putting into practice those many truths that they should have been *learning* for so many years, and that they more recently should have been *learning* how to use in the Junior High period. The Junior High stress on *how to* should culminate in a Senior stress on *doing*.

But, if truth merely has been stored for quick retrieval for the next Bible quiz up to and even during the Junior High period, and there has been little or no instruction or opportunity to use that truth, when young people enter the High School period they cannot be expected to do so automatically. And, since so often they have not been prepared previously as they should have, they do not. It is not enough then to scold them for not doing so; instead what must be done is (1) to give the needed instruction belatedly, (2) against hardened, wrong patterns developed during the more flexible Junior High period, and (3) in spite of the discontent and rebellion that such failure often encourages. This is difficult, not necessary, and frequently unrewarding. It is therefore time to reconsider the Junior High period.

What more specifically, should Junior/Senior Highs be learning/doing? For one thing, they should be discovering how to use their Bibles in the practical manner in which they were intended to be used (cf. II Timothy 3:17 the "scriptures ... are *useful*"). It is one thing to know the catechism answers, to be able to recite favorite Bible portions, or even to know how to turn to key Scriptures to prove doctrinal positions. It is *quite* another to know how to find the scriptural answer to a practical problem encountered at school on Tuesday. Not only do very few Juniors and all-too-few Seniors know how to use the Bible in this way, but many of their parents have never learned to do so either. This skill, above all others, is the crucial one to be taught and learned (in the Junior years) for use in the critical Senior year (when so many vital issues and decisions face them) and beyond. Unless these skills are taught and used, the Bible will become little more than a book of history and impractical pious platitudes to Senior Highs. No wonder many Seniors see no value in the Scriptures — they have been taught to do so.

The other principal area for basic instruction (in Junior years) and for service (in Senior years) involves the discovery, development and deployment of gifts.[2] It is during Junior years that leaders should begin to

---

[2] For more on this see *supra*, Chapter Ten.

emerge and leadership skills should be developed. Persons with musical abilities (both singing and instrumental) should be encouraged to use these for the Lord. The testing of gifts for preaching should begin by providing opportunities for young men to speak and teach. Regular ministry to others both within and without the congregation should take place. What Juniors stumblingly learn to do during those tadpole days, Senior frogs can accomplish with aplomb. And the skills encouraged and learned during both periods will go far toward developing strong church leadership potential of the proper sort for the next generation. Congregations with no such vision sow the seeds of their future destruction. Pastors themselves must promote a vital youth program based (at least) upon these crucial understandings. They cannot sit by idly while wave upon wave of young people move through these periods with their lives unaffected by those things that will count (individually and corporately) for Jesus Christ.

Just a final word must be spoken to emphasize the need during both of these periods for active meaningful youth programs that influence the young people, not only on Sunday, but that also provide weekday Christian fun and fellowship. There are few things more tragic than to discover that so little is happening among the covenant youth during these years when friendship and peer pressure is so important, that many of them make friends and subject themselves to detrimental influences outside of the church. Every pastor must be vigilant to guard and work against any such deficiency. Parents of teenagers desperately need the help that can be provided only by full, vital training in Christian living. Whatever it takes in any congregation to achieve this goal, the pastor must do. He cannot merely deplore a bad state of affairs; he must take action to rectify it.

Finally, a vital growing youth program involves a strong evangelistic effort by the youth of the church. Young people grow most when they serve both one another and the unsaved world around them. A youth group composed only of covenant youth will lack in zeal and reality. It continually must be fed by a life-giving stream of converted unbelievers if it would not become crusty. The faith comes alive to covenant youth growing up in the church where their views and ways are regularly challenged by new converts. The latter keep the former honest; the former help the latter to understand. A good mix of the two is essential for a healthy youth work. Thus, as a significant emphasis of the youth work teaching and programs for doing evangelism must be developed at the Junior High Age and continued through the Senior period. Nothing helps youth come to know their Bibles and their faith better than the need to use both in evangelism.

EXERCISE

For the Student

Make a list of the topics that you might wish to teach children who have been excluded from the worship service in order to prepare them for participation at a later point when they become more mature.

For the Pastor

Take a hard look at your Junior High program. If it is deficient, develop a truly significant program as soon as possible. Give this *high priority*.

CHAPTER FIFTEEN
MAKING THE CHURCH LIBRARY WORK

Let me say it at the outset! When beginning a church library, do not ask for books in general, unless you want to get hundreds of worthless volumes to waste space on your shelves, along with dozens of heretical works to boot. And, don't forget the potential for hurt feelings that this procedure involves, since you will find it necessary to reject most of the junk that is offered. No, in making the appeal for funds and for gift books, see to it that those who are in charge take the trouble to decide and to mimeograph and distribute a list of the books desired. "Volunteerism" in donating furniture, books, etc., is always as bad a policy as when one requests volunteers for jobs around the church. Instead always determine what or who is wanted and go after that.

The library should be located prominently and should be accessible to all. Posters, and/or announcements of new accessions should be made regularly in the congregational newsletter. Posting of book jackets on the library bulletin board under the heading "New Books In Your Library" is one way to announce their arrival. If the jackets become torn and dirty before they are replaced by new ones, that is one possible indication that the library is not acquiring new titles rapidly enough. The library should be financed by the regular church budget, from time to time should make special appeals for large sets (of commentaries, etc.) and should regularly make requests for presentations of specific titles that are out of print. The selection of books placed in the library should be under the direct review of the pastor and the elders. Of course, they may entrust the matter to some doctrinally sound member, perhaps a deacon. Arrangements for other matters pertaining to the functioning of the library should be handed over to the deacons. Older persons, chosen by them, who do not have the gift for other tasks may make fine librarians.

Probably, in setting up a church library, the pastor will have to make the initial effort to determine the basic content of the library. To him also will fall the task of suggesting books all along to the deacon in charge. Review and reports of the health of the library should be made regularly by the deacons to the elders.

The library may promote special programs from time to time in the Church School and in the Youth Groups. These programs may be helpful for alerting members of the congregation to new materials, and for giving instruction and encouragement to the youth of the congregation to read good Christian literature. The library should acquire and feature as many of the *best* children's books as they can afford. Sunday School books, papers and leaflets (which may be bound) ought also to be placed in the Church library. The library may wish to develop and sponsor a Book Club, which might meet monthly to review and to discuss current books.

Cassette tapes and audio visual equipment for use at home or in the church may be assigned to the library to keep tabs on and to promote their use. It is better to assign this equipment to a central unit, like the library, that is already concerned with the problems of record keeping and checking out and checking in, than to assign the task to the Church School. Equipment is less likely to get lost, and to be abused thereby. What is the whole Church's responsibility is no one's responsibility. The library should be open at definite, posted hours. The personnel should be chosen for faithfulness and regularity. Assistants and other back up workers also should be appointed.

EXERCISE

For the Student

1. Make a list of topical headings for use in the beginning of a small church library.
2. Under each topic, list at least five basic books.

For the Pastor

1. Review your church library for junk books, for glaring omissions, and for doctrinally unsound materials. Analyze library use, policies and procedures.

2. Bring a report to the Board of Elders about the state of the library, together with your suggestions for improvement.

CHAPTER SIXTEEN
CHURCH BUILDINGS

Gatherings of the early church were held in private houses,[1] in school buildings[2] or (it seems) wherever it was possible to find a suitable place in which to meet and worship. The Jews had built synagogues (the word means literally "gathering places") all over the Mediterranean world. Jesus and the early missionaries attended services and preached in these buildings in order to proclaim the gospel to those in attendance. While no scriptural directions to build meeting places of any sort exist, it is perfectly clear that (in principle) the New Testament does not oppose the construction and use of church buildings. Nor, it should be observed, does it require them. Buildings, therefore, are viewed solely in a functional manner in the new age. In contrast to the symbolism of the Old Testament Temple, in which the various features, furnishings and functions typified the coming Messiah and His redemption, the New Testament considers both the form of worship,[3] and the building in which it is carried on, something indifferent. A house, a school, a special building constructed specifically for the purpose of worship—all will do. Attempts by Protestants to design church buildings symbolically in order to express Christian truth, therefore are bound to fail. There simply is no philosophy of Christian symbolism in architecture, because the New Testament gives us none. Apart from the most general principles like (1) the importance of good stewardship in construction, (2) doing all things well to the glory of God, and (3) bearing a witness to others by all that we do, there is little more that can be said about the biblical principles concerning church buildings.

It would seem that balance, witness to the community, and function constitute the three prime implications growing out of them. A balance between overexpenditures leading to mismanagement of the Lord's money in poor stewardship (on the one hand), and (on the other) drab, shabby or

---

[1]Romans 16:5; Colossians 4:15; Acts 18:7

[2]Acts 19:9,10.

[3]We shall discuss liturgical matters in a later volume, D.V. Of course, specific directions, in accord with the general principle of order, were given (cf. I Corinthians 14).

uninviting barrenness that turns off the public ought to be struck. Moreover, a combination of the principles of stewardship and function (which points to the principal reason for the investment of funds) demands that the property be designed for use on more than one day per week. Designers should take into consideration the possible weekday use of the building for a Christian School, as furloughed missionary quarters, as office space for Christian organizations, for a Christian bookstore, for daily youth activity, etc. In this way, and in this way alone, can large expenditures for buildings be justified.

Witness too is important. Probably there is no more sad commentary on many Protestant congregations than the shabbiness and unkempt condition of their church buildings. Of course, there are many marvelous exceptions as well. But, no church ought to engage in building unless there are both the will and the resources to keep the building and its environs attractive and in good repair at all times. The condition of the church property is all the witness that some in the community will ever see. I am not referring to ornateness or to any extraordinary expenditure of funds for special features, but simply to the matters of neatness and appearance. Uncut grass (or lawns with bare spots), blistering and peeling paint, poor landscaping, inadequate off-street parking, or a hundred-and-one other factors that lead to the run-down condition of a church say something to the community; but not what the church intended, surely. Gingerbread, like garish signs, illuminated glass brick crosses, and other tasteless touches also say much that was not intended. The elegance of neat simplicity combined with good upkeep tells the community that the congregation cares about God, and about the neighborhood. When the church property is the eyesore of the vicinity, the community gets the opposite message. The love of God and the love of one's neighbor demand concern.

In addition to the church auditorium, the pastor's study and the nursery are two critical areas for special care. The study is a place where many people (members and others) come for counsel. Here is one place where the pastor himself has the opportunity (and obligation) to set and to maintain high standards of excellence for the rest of the congregation, If the study is neat (though not unused), clean, pleasant, etc., it will serve as a model for the congregation in their care of the rest of the building. I mention the nursery because mothers are concerned about finding cleanliness, safety features, and adequate facilities (toilet, sink, cribs) in this room for their infants. When you remember that the church-going habits of many young married couples are formed at this point in their lives, you can recognize the importance of not allowing nursery failures to put unnecessary obstacles in their way, Evident concern for their children is a message that the church nursery *must* convey.[4]

Thus, the church building will bear a good or a bad witness to the honor or dishonor of Christ. There is no neutrality here; the building helps or hinders. It is the task of every pastor to help his elders and deacons to see that the church property is a sharp and effective tool for worship and for witness. While it is not his job to design buildings himself and to do the upkeep that is necessary, it is his duty to stress the principles of stewardship, function and witness that apply. The minister cannot ignore gross failures to show concern about such matters. It is his obligation to alert, educate, encourage and (when necessary) to rebuke those who are responsible for the failure.

The youth room(s) should be decorated by them — not by the church. While certain limits may need to be set, a large amount of freedom should be given to them (to paint, put down multicolored carpet samples on the floor, etc.). They need a place to call their own, and in which they can conduct their meetings and hold their activities with comfort. If they have worked on the room themselves, they will take pride in it, be more likely to spend time in it, and treat it with care.

The Sexton

Most American pastors will not experience either of the extremes for good or ill that some of us have. In my ministry, for instance, I have worked with a slimmed down version of the Scottish Beadle, who turns out to be far more than the church sexton. Indeed, he conceived of himself as my right hand man. He brought cookies and tea every morning during my study period and, in general, tried to serve not only by caring for the building, but also for its occupants. The only things that can be said for such a sexton is that if you ever get one, do not take advantage of him!

On the other hand, at another church, I had a sexton who conceived of himself as the owner and sole proprietor of the premises. This I discovered (to my chagrin) when he sharply took me to task for rearranging the location of some bookshelves in the pastor's study. His words (most of which thankfully I have forgotton) were to the effect that I had rearranged *his building*. To this day those last possessives vividly stand out in my memory.

But, as I say, most will not face either of these extremes. Instead, most

---

[4]Not only by the physical facilities, but also by the personnel who man the nursery. Instruction should be given to every worker in the nursery so that a consistent level of care is maintained.)

sextons will be persons, often hard up for work for one reason or another (the reasons *can* be vital), who normally (but not always) do a reasonably good job of keeping the church neat and clean. A wise pastor will cultivate, not ignore, the church sexton. First, since many others will tend to look down on him, it is the pastor's duty to set a proper example for the rest of the congregation in accordance with James 2:1-9. He must not show favoritism for the rich, well-educated, etc. Secondly, since the upkeep and appearance of the church are of such vital concern to the witness of the church, it is important for the pastor to be on such terms with the sexton that he can encourage him to see to it that this witness does not suffer.

The concern of the pastor for a good relationship with the sexton should not only be direct; it also should be indirect. That is, it should be expressed concretely in personal ways (taking time to sit down and chat — perhaps the pastor himself might start the tea and cookie routine) in showing interest in projects in which the sexton is engaged around the church building, etc., and in other ways as well (urging the congregation to increase his wages, reminding those who are married in the church of the extra time and effort that weddings mean for the sexton, and suggesting that they express their appreciation to him for it in some substantial way, etc.).

A good relationship with the church sexton is of genuine importance to the effective use of the church facilities. Every pastor therefore should work hard to establish and maintain such a relationship.

EXERCISE

For the Student

Drive around and look at the outer community witness of the church buildings of at least 25 evangelical congregations. Note, below, the condition of each, and basic improvements that might be made.

For the Pastor

Who is in charge of the buildings and grounds of your congregation? When did you last consult with him? Could you profitably hold a meeting or two with him to discuss improvements ("You know, Frank, I was thinking that if. . .).

Ideas for Improvement

CHAPTER SEVENTEEN
FINANCES IN THE LOCAL CHURCH

If you expected a long and detailed study of finances in the local church and a thorough discussion of the pastor's prime role in handling them, you will be sadly disappointed. I see no biblical warrant for the pastor to busy himself with the details of church finances. Notice, I said *details*. Instruction in giving and in good stewardship is indeed a vital part of his teaching ministry (a fact that too many pastors forget or conveniently neglect). So crucial is this type of pastoral activity that Paul exhorts Timothy to set up a special rich men's Bible study in order to instruct wealthy persons how to use their money for the honor of Christ (cf. I Timothy 6:6-10; 17-19)! It is tragic to realize how many churches and other Christian organizations suffer precisely because the pastors of wealthy Christians have never taken seriously the charge given to them in verses 17-19.

Yes, the pastor must develop courage to speak generally and to specific individuals about money. It is his job, with Paul, to see that special offerings are taken for worthwhile causes among the people of God. Also like Paul, he will find it necessary to instruct, to exhort, to rebuke and to encourage. When it comes to giving, many Christians show little evidence of sanctification. About his duties in this regard, there can be no question. But it is *not* his duty to determine all of the details of the church budget, to distribute the church's funds personally, to make financial arrangements with visiting speakers and a score of other details. This he and the elders need to leave safely in the hands of the diaconate.

His own giving, again, should set the example for the entire congregation. And, if at times his salary is meager, like the widow, he can give his mite. But, he should also be an example to the flock in the way in which he insists upon an adequate salary for his family.[1] Congregations are notorious for giving insufficient funds to pastors, yet all the while expecting them to keep their homes and their clothes in the best style, and wondering

---

[1]Cf. *Shepherding God's Flock,* Vol. I, pp. 65,68,69.

why they do not run all over the map in a large, respectable car that carries lots of Sunday School children and drinks gasoline. It is time for pastors to summon the courage to tell their boards that all that it takes to support a pastor is ten families giving a tenth. Simple math makes it plain that they easily can give him a salary equal to the average salary of the ten. Monies given by all other families are gravy for the maintenance of the property, missions, etc. Galatians 6:6 makes it clear that the pastor-teacher is to live on a level equal to that of the members of the congregation: The one who is taught is to "share *all good things*" with his teacher. No, it takes no more than simple math *and* the grace of God for the members of a congregation to see this! The church should never be in need of money — especially for the pastor's salary — there ought always to be an excess. The church's problem constantly should take this form: "Where would God have us use these excess funds?" It is not many people who are needed to support the ministry of a local congregation financially; it just takes a few *dedicated* families to do so.[2]

EXERCISE

For the Student

1. Determine how much money it will take for you to live and take care of your family (if not yet married, postulate a wife and one child) in your first pastorate. Interview several pastors for help in this matter.

2. Call up the local I.R.S. office and ask about the best way of breaking down a minister's salary (e.g., is it better to ask for a manse allowance, car allowance, book allowance, utilities allowance, etc., than to receive the same amount as straight salary?).

3. Be prepared to report on your findings.

---

[2]New congregations should be declared to be *congregations* only (1) when they are self-supporting (ten families giving a tenth) or the equivalent thereof. . . but, the stress should be upon proper giving by *all* from the outset, and (2) when they have adequate elder material to form a board of elders. Prior to this, the pastor (to be) and the congregation are in a missionary relationship.

For the Pastor

1. What have you done in general to give financial instruction to your members?

2. To those who are rich? (Or have you been afraid to approach them about the use of their wealth for Christ?)

3. What should you do about each?

CHAPTER EIGHTEEN
PUBLICITY

It is sad to scan the columns of a newspaper searching for the location of the congregation of God's people that you wish to visit, only to find that this church does not advertise. Yet, there on the religious news page is the ad for every liberal church and every cult in town. Far too many Bible believing pastors, who ought to be the first to recognize the value of promoting the work of Christ through the media, seem never to have given serious thought to the variety of legitimate ways and means that are available. For instance, in inquiring about information from the local Chamber of Commerce of a city to which you intend to move, you may receive a letter from three or four congregations in that city. Why didn't the one in which you especially were interested also write? The answer again: because that congregation has missed the publicity opportunity.

Publicity is not sub-christian. Some of those who piously decry the use of publicity, do so, I fear, in order to excuse their lethargy. Yet, God sent John the Baptist "before" Jesus to *prepare* a people for him. That preparation involved much more, of course, but in it was the element of publicity: John announced, "The Kingdom is at hand." He spoke of the One who would come after him, and gathered together a people who were expectant (Luke 3:15). Here is an example of the highest level publicity: it prepares people to expectantly meet Christ. It did so by announcing the facts about the coming of the Messiah. The work of the Seventy was a kind of publicity effort too, whatever else it may have had in view. Publicity, then, when accurate, honest, appropriate and Christ-centered is scriptural. Publicity, in general, must not be equated with the sensationalism, the exaggeration, and the fraudulent misrepresentations that have characterized much American religious publicity. It is because of this abuse of publicity that a seemingly reasonable case against publicity has been made. But all good things (sex, preaching, etc.) may be abused. That is no argument against them, when *properly* used.

Publicity has characterized some of the more effective ministries that truly honor God and His Son. We must not throw away the package with its torn wrapper.

There are many ways in which to publicize the work of a local congregation, and I shall not attempt to list or categorize all of them. Rather, I wish to stimulate the pastor to think through the ways in which he can promote the use of good publicity both within and without his congregation.

To begin with, it is important to encourage every organization within the church to appoint someone (with the gifts to do so) to publicize the work of that organization. These are the church Reporters. The elders should see to it that the deacons handle all of the general publicity for the church, and that they supervise the publicity of the other organizations of the church. Whoever is appointed by the deacons to the position of Head Reporter for the church should be capable of offering helpful suggestions to the other organizational Reporters. These suggestions may include help about what to publicize, ways and means to do so, how to get better circulation of publicity, and how to coordinate it with other publicity that is going into or coming out of the church. He should instruct these Reporters in the use of news releases and provide them with a supply of News Release forms. The pastor, in turn, may from time to time make suggestions to the Head Reporter, who acts as general coordinator, and may encourage him to see that others responsible for publication produce acceptable publicity and do not fail to seize opportunities.

Public Media

A key factor in publicity is the local newspaper. This, along with radio and TV stations should be used as fully as possible and that does not mean merely to rent space and time for paid advertisements. Particularly in small towns and cities (but not only there) it is possible to obtain *much* more space for the local church than the average church has any idea. Free time on local radio stations, opportunities for interviews (especially of visiting speakers) on TV shows, and many other public media possibilities exist. Yet, only a few pastors enter into these in an adequate way.

Upon beginning a new pastorate, one of the first things any pastor should do is to make appointments with the public media representative that he will be working with in his new community in order to get acquainted and to discuss the best ways and means to assure the best cooperation. For this appointment the pastor should offer to take the representative to lunch (funds for such luncheons should be paid out of the pastor's yearly contingency fund, provided by the church for all such occasions[1]). In this interview, the pastor should be ready to make some promises that he is willing to keep. In many communities, the Religious Editor is paid by the word. He (or she) *wants news* and is more interested, therefore, in feature articles and basic newsworthy material than in the announcements that appear in the paid-for columns. The pastor must assure this editor that, unlike many of the pastors with whom he or she has worked in the past (and they will tell you that pastors have bad records) who promise, but fail to deliver, he will keep the news coming in a steady flow. There is nothing that could make the editor happier than this; it is his (her) bread-and-butter. Moreover, he should make it clear that he will do all that he can to inform the editor of conventions or other special features of the programs of his church that may merit special coverage (such as a reporter and photographer on hand), far enough in advance to make plans for it. Furthermore, he will see to it that a *written description* of each week's meetings (not merely an announcement of each) will be sent for the newspaper's Church News column, together with glossy pictures of any noteworthy persons that the church may bring to town. In order to impress upon the editor that he means business, he may hand to him a copy of the mimeographed News Release that he intends to use. This may be discussed so that (1) any modifications necessary may be made; (2) both understand its full purpose. A copy of this follows:

---

[1]If there is no such fund, here (at the outset) is an occasion for requesting it.

8½"

NEWS RELEASE

_____ Church

Address_____

Phone _____

1. For immediate release _____ .
2. For release on

_____ .

3. For release at any time _____ .

11"

Subject:

Released by _____

The Reporters from each organization also must be encouraged to be faithful in sending information. Probably such information should be sent to the church-appointed Head Reporter, who in turn (perhaps in consultation with the pastor from time to time) will edit and revise and send in, compound news releases, containing all of the significant facts about each organization in a blended form.

Printing is expensive, mimeographing is less so. The local church will find that a used multilith machine and an IBM typewriter with paper masters will produce fine looking materials at a cost only slightly higher than the cost of mimeographing. Church bulletins, brochures of all sorts, tracts, pamphlets, cards, announcements, etc., all can be produced by the use of a multilith. However, it is essential to find someone (or a couple of persons) within the congregation who will be willing to spend the time and the effort to learn how to operate the machine well and who will view their continued work in printing as a ministry. It can become an enormous asset to the local church. This printing press will, in time, not only pay for itself many times over, but will provide attractive materials for use in every phase of the congregational activities.

EXERCISE

For the Student and the Pastor

Together with no more than five other pastors[2] (students) brainstorm new ways of publicizing the work of the church. Procedures:

1. Brainstorm for one hour.
2. A secretary should record ideas *during* the one hour session.
4. Piggy-back on each other's ideas.
5. Following the session jointly and/or individually evaluate each idea scripturally and practically (if scriptural, is it feasible or workable for my congregation?).
6. Record all acceptable ideas below.

---

[2]Perhaps in a presbyterial gathering with several small groups.

CHAPTER NINETEEN
CONCLUSION

I do not wish to make this chapter any longer than necessary. Therefore, rather than sum up in some other way, I have determined to challenge you with one final summary exercise. It is a test. There are only twenty-five questions; that means that normally you would grade each question with a weight of 4 on a scale of 100. But, your Lord does not settle for 50's and 60's, or even 80's. He says "be perfect." Therefore, grade each question with a weight of 100! Until you can answer each His way, you have changes to make. I think you will find the Check List provocative.

A Pastoral Leadership Check List
1. Do I run a one man show?
2. Do I allow my decisions to be influenced by pressure?
3. Do I exercise biblical leadership, or do I sense the direction of the prevailing winds and go in that direction?
4. Have I concentrated on discovering, developing and deploying the gifts of others?
5. Do I tend to shirk responsibility whenever possible?
6. Do I run or compromise when the going gets tough?
7. Am I complacent? Discouraged? Weary from well doing?
8. Do I have a desire for self glory?
9. Do I love my people? If not, what am I doing to cultivate that love?
10. Do I know the problems and the needs among the flock? Do I know what to do about these? Am I doing something?
11. Is there adequate communication in the congregation? Do I know? If not, what does that indicate?
12. Is my time properly organized? By priorities? By whom?
13. Is my life a vital example to my flock?
14. Do I know how to lead rather than drive my flock?
15. Am I using/misusing/not using the authority that Christ gave to me?
16. Do I set goals and plan my work to meet them?

17. Am I trapped by formality, custom and tradition?
18. Am I personally growing in my relationship to God?
19. Do I faithfully work at administration in my congregation?
20. Do I believe in doing administrative work?
21. How do I need to improve as an administrator?
22. Do the members of my congregation look to me as a leader? If not, why?
23. How many hours per month do I spend in committee meetings?
24. What do I do when I run into problems with members of the congregation?
25. How do I encourage the expression of differences of opinion while discouraging personal differences?

APPENDIX A
EVANGELISM AND THE PASTOR

While, strictly speaking, evangelism might not be considered an element essential to this volume because it involves the outreach of a congregation (and individual members from it) to the unconverted community in which God has placed it; nevertheless, there are so many pastoral leadership functions connected with congregational evangelism (planning, guiding, teaching, etc.) that it would be a mistake to avoid the subject. This is true, especially because of the dominant part that evangelism plays in the life of a Christian and of the Church. Moreover, the pastoral effects of evangelism are substantial. A healthy church requires a continual mix of covenantally raised converts with those converted from raw paganism. The former bring a background and heritage to that mix while the latter "keep them honest" by their questions, observations, etc.

It is also important to note that *as the Shepherd* Jesus came to "seek and to save" those who were lost,[1] He has "other sheep" than those from the "house of Israel" (John 10:16). Thus, pastors, as Christ's undershepherds who care for the flock, should be vitally concerned to increase the flock, and in particular, to encourage the evangelistic fervor of every member of the congregation. The pastor must be in the vanguard of every such effort, constantly doing all that he can to bring about a congregational concern and capability for the work.

In order to enable the pastor to lead his flock into an evangelistic outreach into the community, I shall sketch out (in *some* detail) a congregational visitation evangelism/Bible study plan that I have used successfully and that other congregations also have found useful.

The fundamental biblical presuppositions behind this plan are three:

    1. Evangelism is the work of the *whole* congregation; it is not the task of the pastor only.

---

[1]Luke 19:10, Ezekiel 34:6 ("there was no one to seek them"), 8 (they "did not search"), 11 (" myself will search for my sheep and seek them out"), 16 ("I will seek the lost, bring back the scattered"). Cf. Zechariah 11:16 in which the worthless shepherd is contrasted as one wh "will not seek the scattered or heal the wounded." Cf. also Jeremiah 23:3,4: "I . . . shall brin them back to their pasture" and "nor will any be missing."

2. Evangelism, like other Christian tasks, must be taught by the discipleship (or modeling) method,[2] and the pastor is the principal (though not sole) teacher/model.

3. Evangelism involves a full presentation of the gospel (and nothing less) that may require time and continued contact, and is not done properly by hit-and-run methods.

Let us then see how these three elements may direct a combined visitation evangelism and Bible study approach. This program may be used in a small congregation, in a very large one or when attempting to begin a new congregation.

The program is entitled:

Everyone Evangelizing Everywhere[3]

It is based upon Acts 8:4 "Therefore, those who were scattered abroad, went everywhere announcing the message of good news" (a literal translation). The following materials have been developed for use in training participants in the program. Other materials (referred to in them) are for use in the evangelistic enterprise itself.

The Instructional Materials

Leader's Manual

You are the key to this Visitation Evangelism Program. It is a program that involves the spiritual welfare of many persons. In your particular congregation it can mean the beginnings of a revival and new spiritual growth for your people. And of equal importance — its great purpose is the salvation of souls.

This plan has been tested in a number of communities and shown to be effective in reaching men for Christ. But will this approach succeed in your community? This may depend largely upon the faithful preparation and presentation that you are willing to give it. If it is to be effective, you must be willing to spend the necessary time in study and preparation. Work hard! Only then can you fully understand the way it works and direct others in carrying it out. Don't even think of starting unless you are willing to face this task with enthusiasm and dedication. Your vigorous leadership is necessary for stirring enthusiasm in others. Anything less will fail.

---

[2]Cf. *Competent to Counsel,* Chapter 11, *The Big Umbrella,* Chapter 12, and *The Christian Counselor's Manual,* pp. 332ff.

[3]The materials for this Visitation Evangelism program are available from the publisher of this Volume. A *V.E. Packet,* containing a *Leader's Manual,* 200 *How To Do* Manuals, 25 *Teacher's Guides,* 1000 *Inserts,* 1000 *V-Cards* and 100 *Student's Workbooks* (H.B.S. Workbooks) is available at a special price.

The pastor or an elder in an established congregation ordinarily will be the leader of the Visitation Evangelism Program. If the church has not yet been established, and has no pastor or elders, the leader should be the most enthusiastic and well versed member of the nucleus of interested people. The materials, however, have been written in such a way that each person who participates may readily understand the work to be done at his level. Every effort has been made to be clear and simple.

The plan also calls for completeness. This means that, without becoming complicated, the materials are comprehensive. The leader will find, therefore, that he will be greatly aided by following the *entire* program *exactly* as it is presented. This is necessary because it hangs together as a *whole*. It cannot be used as successfully in part. If you find the program too "ambitious" or "rigorous," it might be better not to use it at all. A half-hearted effort is almost certain to fail and bring unnecessary discouragement to you and your people. You will find, though, that the program is really worth all the time and effort that you can invest.

THE CONCEPT OF CONCENTRATION is central to the whole plan. The idea is to work in a concentrated way with a few people for a number of weeks. This also means that your work would be confined to a relatively small territory. In contrast to the shallow hop-skip-and-jump methods of survey campaigns and the hit-and-run nature of some Visitation Evangelism programs, this one sets up the goal of at least eight successive visits in one home: the initial call, the return call, and the six-week Home Bible Study Course.

Though the key concept of concentration must be maintained at all times, the plan is extremely flexible in application. The leader must organize the campaign along lines that fit his own situation. The number of teams and the choice of the area to be covered will depend upon local factors. Any number of visitors, from one up, may engage in this program. Naturally, the elaborateness of the planning will depend upon the number of workers participating. In organized churches, the program may be set up with the pastor as leader. Under him the Board of Elders will head teams composed of members of the congregation. Usually the number of teams will correspond to the number of session members. In unorganized groups the approach should be similar, but in such circumstances it is likely that there will be only one team and one captain.

THE JOB of the leader is sixfold. He must:

1. Inspire the group (especially the Board of Elders) to adopt and support the plan.

2. Mark out the territories and fields, designing and mimeographing maps for all participants.
3. Confer with team captains, instructing them in their duties and apportioning to them the membership of their teams and the territories to be covered.
4. Instruct the visitors and teachers how to do visitation, using the *How To Do* manual as the basic textbook.
5. Supervise and guide the entire program while in process, assisting wherever his help is required.
6. Receive, file, and study all V-cards after each campaign is completed.

The team captains should be elders or other capable persons who are able to assume and carry out responsibilities. Each captain should first survey the "Territory" apportioned to his team, noting the relative lengths of various streets and the number of houses involved. The captain should then divide his team into equal "Fields" and assign each member of his team to a particular Field. Note: This preliminary survey work should be complete *before* the opening day of the campaign. Maps of the whole area should be made and displayed. Maps are also valuable aids for working in the Territory and the Field.

In larger groups, the elders, or whoever the captains may be, will teach the six-week Home Bible Study Courses while the rest of the members make initial visits and return calls. This arrangement is adaptable to local conditions, and it is even possible for the same person to visit as well as teach. The *Teacher's Guide* explains how to use *The Student's Workbook* most effectively. Each teacher should have one.

The team captains, therefore, are expected to teach the six-week Bible course in the home. Teaching, however, must be done by the leader as well as by the team captains. It is the leader's job to teach each captain and team how to carry out the program. This initial teaching of those doing the calling is crucial. In cases where there is more than one team, a separate teaching session for each captain and his teams should be conducted. This also enables people who may not be able to come one night to attend another evening. As much as possible, of course, team members should try to attend the evening allotted to their own team. This keeps the instruction period small and informal and initiates team spirit. Incidentally, new members, brought into the church by the program, may well want to be assigned to the team which contacted them.

THIS TEACHING CLASS for the teams should be two hours long. The first hour should be pure *instruction* without discussion. The next half hour, *illustration*. Following , this, there should be a five minute *intermission*. And finally, the closing twenty-five minutes (or less) may be thrown open for *inquiry* and discussion. Adhere firmly to this schedule.

I. *Instruction* (by the Leader)

Begin with instruction with theory. The visitor's *How To Do* manual will be the basis for this instruction. You may want to begin by writing the four main points on the blackboard (Instruction, Illustration, Intermission, Inquiry), and by explaining the reasons for this procedure. Immediately assure the class that ample time will be provided at the close for any questions that remain unanswered. But insist that they be withheld until then. Suggest that they jot them down in their notebooks so that they won't forget them. Explain that there is much to cover under theory and that most questions will be answered there and in the illustrative period.

By way of general instruction, explain the principles found in the Introduction to the *Leader's Manual*. And more specifically, present and interpret the material found in the *How To Do* manual. (Distribute copies of the *How To Do* manual to the students at the beginning of the instruction period and use it as an outline. Since repetition is helpful in teaching, it won't hurt for them to hear it from the leader and later to read it from the manual. The leader, certainly, has the liberty to expand and explain in his own words, but in order to avoid confusion, he should be careful to preserve the uniform terminology employed in all the literature (e.g., "Return Call, Field, Householder," etc.).

In teaching, a blackboard, charts, maps, and sample copies of the materials should be employed as visual aids.

II. *Illustration*

"At the door" problems, and how to handle them. (This is a study in visiting principles and techniques.)

Introduction

The following situations have been exaggerated somewhat in order to make the principles stand out. They should be acted out to demonstrate proper and improper techniques. The effect may be heightened by the construction of a frame doorway. Supports, purporting to be railings, are an attractive means of holding the door and its frame upright. Of course, normal doorway may be used.

The characters in this dialogue are: *Narrator* (part taken by the leader), *Householder* (woman), visitor (man), and *Sound Effects Man.*

Props: Frame doorway, wet spaghetti mop, bucket full of water, briefcase containing Visitation Evangelism literature, and Bible.

Nothing is more important than the initial contact. First impressions are lasting. Failure here often destroys all opportunity to witness later. That is why this section of the training program is so necessary. You will find that it stimulates real interest and is a great help to your visitors. *Don't fail to use it.* Be sure your actors rehearse and learn their parts thoroughly. If the actors ham it up ä bit, that's good so long as the point of each skit is not obscured thereby.

The leader (narrator) begins by announcing:

Three fundamental principles to be remembered are:
1. Establish and maintain rapport.
2. Consider every objection a challenge to be overcome.
3. Be flexible.

Situation No. 1

A. Wrong:

Narrator: You are about to observe the acting out of the first situation. Initially, it will be handled incorrectly, then repeated in a proper way. Watch carefully, and try to determine what main principle the visitor has forgotten. It would be advisable to take notes.

(Visitor appears on the scene carrying briefcase and Bible. Knocks on door. After a moment's pause, disheveled lady appears with spaghetti mop in one hand and bucket of water in other. She is obviously in the midst of housework, and appears quite disturbed by the interruption. She speaks:)

Householder: Yeah? Whadda *you* want?

Visitor: How do you do? My name is Cuthbert Cobblestone. I'm from the new church that ...

Householder: (Who hasn't heard a word he said, since she has been looking over her shoulder) Say, Joe, Will you pin those diapers on the baby?

Sound Effects Man: (Answers from offstage) Oh, all right.

Householder: (Looking at visitor at last) What didj'a say?

Visitor: How do you do? My name is Cuthbert Cobblestone. I'm from the new church that is being built on Baker Street. I'm visiting in this neighborhood today to ...

Sound Effects: (Baby lets out shriek and continues to cry from off stage while exasperated householder says:)

Householder: I'm sorry mister, I gotta' go. He's pinned the diaper to the baby again! (She slams door)

Narrator: Horrors! Wasn't that terrible? What important *principle* did the visitor forget? (Here entertain responses) Yes, the visitor was guilty of a common fault — INFLEXIBILITY. Just as no two doors look exactly alike, so no two doors will present the same situation. Visitors must be flexible, ready to meet any situation. Let's do it again; only this time, the right way.

   B. Right:

(Visitor knocks on door, and a woman opens with same props as first time)

Visitor: Oh! It looks like you're really busy today!

Householder: You can say *that* again!

Visitor: I can appreciate your being busy, and I won't disturb you. I have something important to discuss with you. When will you be free to talk? Would four o'clock this afternoon be a better time?

Householder: Important? Well ... I guess you could come back about four o'clock this afternoon.

Visitor: Fine, I'll see you then. Goodbye.

Householder: (Remains in doorway leaning on mop, and muses:) Important? I wonder what that could be.

Narrator: Well, that's more like it! Now let's look at a different problem. See if you can detect the forgotten principle here. First, let's look at it incorrectly handled.

Situation No. 2

   A. Wrong:

(Visitor approaches door as before and knocks. Woman householder appears)

Householder: Yes?

Visitor: How do you do? My name is Cuthbert Cobblestone. I'm from the new church that is being built on Baker Street. I'm visiting in this community today to get acquainted with our future neighbors, tell them something about our church, and what we believe.[4] May I come in?

Householder: Thanks anyway, but I've got my religion.

Visitor: Oh ... I see ... Uh ... Ah ... Well ... Goodbye.

---

[4]The words "and what we believe" are important; they make what you do later on ethically justifiable.

(Visitor walks off; woman closes door)

Narrator: Pretty sad! What was wrong here? What principle was forgotten? (Here entertain responses) Right, the principle here is: CONSIDER EVERY OBJECTION A CHALLENGE TO BE OVERCOME! He gave up far too easily. No salesman would do that. Let's see how we might overcome that argument.

B. Right:

Householder: Yes?

Visitor: (Here he repeats exact speech as above)

Householder: Thanks anyway, but I've got my religion.

Visitor: Oh, I see. Well, I'm certainly glad to meet you. It's good to meet someone who is really interested in religion. You'd be surprised how many people I've talked to who don't seem interested at all.

Householder: (In a tone, already softened) Is that so?

Visitor: Definitely! I know *you especially* will be interested in hearing something about our new church. May I have a few minutes of your time?

Householder: (Somewhat hesitantly at first) Why yes, won't you come in?

(Visitor enters; door closes)

Narrator: Very nicely done! But what made the difference? The first visitor allowed the objection to become a barrier and gave up; the second one considered it a challenge, and *turned the objection itself into a stepping stone* by which he gained entrance. How did he convert a liability into an asset? Note this: write it down—and never forget it: *HE FOUND SOMETHING IN THE OBJECTION THAT HE COULD HONESTLY COMMEND.* This is very important. Now, let's consider one final situation.

Situation No. 3

A. Wrong:

(Visitor knocks at door as previously; a woman answers)

Householder: Yes?

Visitor: (Here he repeats exact speech as above)

Householder: I'm not interested. I go to the Catholic Church.

Visitor: That's a shame!

Householder: What do you mean, *Sir?*

Visitor: Just this. (Pointing and shaking finger at woman) The trouble with you Romanists is that you worship Mary and the saints instead of God. And that's not all ...

Householder: (Breaks in indignantly) Well! I've heard just about enough! (Slams door in his face)

Narrator: Well, he certainly deserved it! I don't have to point out to you that he lost *rapport* immediately by launching into an argument. His language, manner, and approach were all antagonistic. The Bible speaks of the "offense of the cross," but that is quite different from the offense of the visitor. Let's see one way that he could have dealt with this common problem.

B. Right:
(Visitor knocks at door; woman answers)
Householder: Yes?
Visitor: (Here he repeats same opening speech)
Householder: I'm not interested. I go to the Catholic Church.
Visitor: I see! I am certainly happy to meet someone with religious convictions. There are so *few* people who have any convictions today.
Householder: (With noticeably renewed interest) That's right.
Visitor: We are glad that the Vatican Council encouraged discussion between persons of all religions. I'd like to hear *your opinion* on one or two questions and *explain some of our beliefs.* May I come in for a moment?
Householder: Well ... I suppose it *would* be interesting. Come on in.
Visitor: Thank you. (He enters)

END

III *Intermission*

Following the Illustration period there should be a brief five-minute intermission for the people to move about and talk—cookies and coffee might help. Call the group to order promptly at the end of the five minutes.

IV *Inquiry*

The final twenty-five minutes should be reserved for questions and discussion as promised. Here the Leader should be prepared to answer any reasonable question about the program that may be asked. It is essential for him to have a thorough familiarization with all aspects of the program, and all of the materials.

HOW TO DO VISITATION EVANGELISM
(An Instruction Manual for Field Workers)

The How To Manual (Every visitor gets a copy)

Introduction

The need for evangelism is plain. Christ said "go"; few if any come seeking. Therefore, the gospel must be *taken* to them. Evangelism can be done *occasionally* (as the occasions arise or as individual Christians make them) or it may be done according to a *program*, by the members of a congregation. Either way we must go: Acts 8:4 says that "Those who were scattered abroad *went* ...." The duty is also clear: Evangelism is not a special work for special persons to do at special times. It is not an *extra*, but a basic task of the whole church. The evangelism in Acts 8:4 was carried on by every day man-in-the-pew Christians (driven out of Jerusalem in the providence of God on an evangelistic mission). This is clear because Acts 8:1 indicates that all were scattered abroad *"except the apostles."* The leadership was not included in that first congregation-wide evangelism effort. Presenting the gospel is one thing that every Christian is capable of doing. Anyone who knows enough to be saved, knows enough to evangelize another. That is why this program carries the word *Everyone* in its title.

Purpose

This program has two goals (the same two set forth in Matthrew 23:19, 20:

1. *Evangelism:* Witnessing to lost men and women for the purpose of discipling them to Christ through faith in Him. They must repent of their sin and believe the gospel (The gospel is summarized in I Corinthians 15:3:"... that Christ died for our sins according to the Scriptures, that he was buried, and that he rose again on the third day according to the Scriptures"). The word gospel means "good news." Evangelizing is "announcing the message of good news" (Acts 8:4).
2. *Edification:* These disciples are to be brought into fellowship with the church, signifying and sealing their membership in that body by water baptism. In this fellowship they must be taught "to observe" (not merely to know) all the things that Christ "commanded." Some evangelistic programs neglect one of these two goals for the sake of the other. This should not be. The effort here is to emphasize both

properly. The visitor first goes to explain the gospel; afterwards, he confronts every convert with his obligation and need to unite with the church.

Preparation

Before each visitation check out these items:
1. Have I studied the Bible, marking key passages for use and memorizing the substance of the passages and the Book and Chapter in which they are located (do not bother to memorize verses or verse numbers).
2. Have I prayed for the salvation of those to whom I shall go?
3. Is my own relationship to God what it should be?
4. Do I have my pen, Bible, tracts, publicity literature and V-cards?
5. Do I know exactly where I am going and what I intend to say?

Theory Of The Visit

Each visitor is assigned one *Field* consisting of a given number of houses for which he is responsible. Each house should be visited at the convenience of the visitor. Visits may be made at night or during the daytime. They may be made by one concentrated effort in one week, or throughout the seven-week period of the campaign. They should be completed by the expiration date. *But*, it is more important to do a thorough job than to visit the entire field. The idea is to cover a limited number of homes intensively. That is, we want to continue working in each home as long as possible. The emphasis is upon depth rather than breadth. One may visit alone, or with another, as he chooses.[5] In the latter case, where persons may wish to assist one another such arrangements should be made informally, but one visitor must assume responsibility for a particular field. NH (not home) listings should be revisited until contact is made. If the field work must be abandoned before completion, contact and inform the elder or district supervisor immediately. V-cards should be filled in fully with special care. Unless the evaluation is clear and concise, the V-cards are of no help for the follow-up program.

Return calls are a very essential part of the program. Every effort must be made to arrange for them. If possible, set the date for sometime during the following week. Make certain to agree upon A DEFINITE

---

[5]There are certain advantages to solo visitation: More territory can be covered in less time, the householder does not feel "ganged up" upon, in a 1 to 1 encounter he is more likely to speak frankly (a third person always becomes an audience). There is, of course, an advantage to duet visitation: an inexperienced worker can be trained in this manner. This is the basic method for training new visitors: they should be discipled by experienced visitors. But visitors, when working together, must learn not to interrupt one another or divert any line of thought which is being pursued.

TIME AND DATE. On the Return Call, the gospel should be discussed more fully and if possible an endeavor may be made to help the householder to come to faith in Christ.

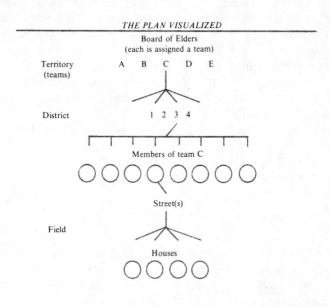

THE PLAN VISUALIZED

Board of Elders
(each is assigned a team)

Territory (teams)   A   B   C   D   E

District   1 2 3 4

Members of team C

Street(s)

Field

Houses

TWO PLANS OF EVANGELISM

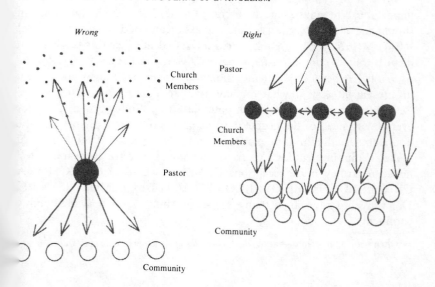

Wrong

Church Members

Pastor

Community

Right

Pastor

Church Members

Community

According to the usual plan, the local church hires a minister to do its work of evangelism and edification. This is impossible. It is a fulltime task to be pastor and teacher of the flock, and no one man can possibly hope to reach the multitudes himself. It is simply a mathematical absurdity. Truly, the pastor is "in the middle." In taking upon himself the work his congregation should do, a minister spreads himself too thinly and does neither his work nor theirs well.

According to the biblical plan, the pastor and teacher is just that. He instructs and inspires the congregation to assume its own evangelistic responsibility. In this way, the task becomes a mathematical possibility. This does not mean that as a Christian the pastor refuses to evangelize. He must be a leader and an example, but he is not a substitute for his congregation.

VISITATION PROPER

VISITATION itself is not very difficult. Getting started is the hardest part. If you prayerfully desire to assume your Christian responsibility to carry the gospel to the lost, soon you will find yourself enjoying the work and becoming adept at it.

Introducing yourself at the door. The first 30 seconds are most important. "Introduce" means literally "to lead into." The introduction should lead into the subject of your discussion and lead you into the house! REMEMBER: the householder was interested in other things when you disturbed him. Your *immediate goal* is to overcome the negative feeling he probably has because of the intrusion and to lead his thoughts away from his present interests to what you have to offer. Your *attitude* is important. Be positive; consider everyone a potential sheep. Smile! Smile! Consider everyone in need of the gospel until he proves otherwise. Be brief on the doorstep. Usually this is no place to witness. Try to get in. If you can't, then make an appointment for a visit at a later date. Leave literature at EVERY house, regardless of the reception.[6] CONSIDER EVERY OBJECTION A CHALLENGE TO BE OVERCOME TACTFULLY. MOST CAN BE. Don't give up any sooner than a salesman would. Look neat. Be humbly confident.

---

[6]Often people, uninterested at the time, have picked up the materials at a later point and read with real interest.

When the householder responds, introduce yourself (and any companion) by name. Say something like this, "How do you do? My name is John Jones. I am from Smithville Church, the NEW church that is being built on Baker Street. (Advertising studies prove that the word "new" is the most important word in selling appeal. People like to hear about something new. If you can do so honestly, work the word into the initial introduction.) I'm visiting in your community today to get acquainted with our future neighbors and to tell you something about our church *and what we believe* (be sure to add this phrase; it is the ethical justification for presenting the gospel). May I come in for a few moments? (At this point move toward the door expectantly.) If the campaign is conducted in an entirely new area, where there is no church yet established, the opening words might be: "How ... I represent the _____ Church. We are going to begin a NEW church in this community. I'm visiting ... etc."

If the householder is busy, or circumstances indicate that a visit at this time would be inappropriate, say something like this: "I appreciate the fact that you are busy. So I don't want to disturb you. When may I return to talk to you?" Then, set a definite time and date, perhaps later on in the same day. Remember, NO TWO DOORS WILL BE THE SAME. Be flexible. (Here typical situations may be acted out.)[7]

NOW THAT YOU ARE IN,[8] what comes next? Upon entering, stand still until invited to take a seat. Be friendly. Relax! Tension causes barriers. Expect to have a good time and you probably will. Take a brief interest in the children or some other pleasantry. But do so sincerely, not hypocritically. If TV sound annoys, get it turned off diplomatically. Speak softly, so that the householder has difficulty hearing you and becomes aware that the TV is a hindrance. Don't waste time on small talk. Get down to business. Here is one way to begin:

"Our church is the _____ Church. (The name of your church may sound like an off-brand. Since you will have to tell him sooner or later that you are from this church, it is best to emphasize your liabilities from the beginning so that you may turn them to advantage. Otherwise the householder may use them to your disadvantage). The reason that we use this name is not because there is anything strange about our church, but because unlike many churches today, we still believe the Bible to be the Word of God.

---

[7]See the brief skit describing ways of handling objections at the door in the *Leader's Manual.*

[8]In this section a fairly full presentation of the gospel is given. This presentation may be adapted to given situations. Scripture verses that teach each point are included; not all may (or should) be used in every presentation.

(That's enough on Liberalism for now; you'll have a much better occasion to deal with it in detail in the H.B.S.[9] course under the Doctrine of the church.)

For instance, we believe the Bible when it says that "all have sinned and come short of the glory of God" (Romans 3:23). You can probably quote this from memory—but don't! Read it from your Bible, so that the householder may see that it actually comes from God's Word. That includes you and me, as well as everyone else. It also tells us that heaven is an absolutely holy place from which all sin is excluded. Sin is breaking God's laws. Therefore, it is an offense against God himself. We have all sinned and this puts us in a difficult position with God. Sin would "defile" heaven, and God says He will not allow this (read Revelation 21:27a). This means, that, because of our sin, none of us can go to heaven. Furthermore the Bible says that He will punish sinners in hell (Matthew 25:46). I am sure that you don't want to go to hell and that you want to go to heaven, don't you? (Often it is helpful to ask questions which you suspect the hearer will answer affirmatively. This tends to create a more favorable atmosphere for conversation). Well, that's one reason why God gave us the Bible—to explain how people can get to heaven in spite of their sin (II Timothy 3:15). The Bible is a record about Christ. It tells how He came into the world to solve the problem of sin. (Here you may read Matthew 1:21 to confirm your statement.) Christ solves the problem of sin by taking man's guilt and punishment upon Himself. When He died on the cross, He was dying in the place of sinners. He became their substitute (I Corinthians 15:3 is one among many texts that prove this). The Bible says that every one who believes that Christ died for his sins and rose from the dead will be saved from hell and go to heaven. His sins will be forgiven, and his faith will be counted for righteousness (Romans 10:9 and other verses in Romans are good here).

"It is not doing good works, joining a church or going through ceremonies that makes a person fit for heaven. Only the death and resurrection of Christ can do that. When I became a Christian, all that could or needed to do was to trust in what He did for me. (Here, you give your own witness to what Christ has done for you. At this point Ephesians 2:8,9 may be useful.) In the Gospel of John (Saint John, if you are speaking to a Roman Catholic) the word "believe" occurs over 90 times. Faith is the one thing that God requires. To believe (or have faith) means to *depend* upon what Christ has done. I wonder if *you* have ever understood an

---

[9]H.B.S. = Home Bible Study.

believed this message before?" (Be sure to end on a question of this sort which will lead the householder to express himself in such a way that you may determine what he thinks and thus what to say next).

From this point on, the discussion (which, by the way, *YOU should be directing* to the goals that *you* have in view) may take almost any turn.[10] Ask enough questions that you may find out exactly what the person believes will get him to heaven, so that you may dispel all false notions and show how this comes through dependence upon the work of Christ alone. Don't overtalk. Ask questions until you think you know enough to see clearly what the householder's problems are. Do not turn off the householder by your questions or remarks. Try to avoid unnecessary argumentation; instead *discuss* points. Stick closely to the main questions of sin, hell, heaven, and salvation through the gospel of Christ. Close the discussion with prayer when appropriate. If the householder seems open, lead him to trust Christ as Savior by praying a simple prayer that you may word for him. Do not push too hard on this initial visit. Especially do not try to push anyone into a decision to believe; let others indicate to you when they are ready to do so. It is important to maintain good relations so that you may return a second time.

Most persons are not ready to believe on the first visit. Go as far as you can in the discussion but no further. Become sensitive to people. Flexibility means that you may not be able to say and do all that is suggested here. Learn how to adapt to each situation.

Arranging for the return call. Regardless of the response to the initial visit, your major goal at this point is to arrange for the Return Call. Future contacts will depend upon success or failure here.

You will have with you three distinct pieces of visitation literature: Several copies of "The _____ Church Invites You ...,"[11] the "Inserts,"[12] and one sample copy of the H.B.S. Workbook.[13] This literature is designed as an aid to assist you in arranging for Return Calls. Learn to use it skillfully.

---

[10]Sometimes the householder will raise a large question. It is often advantageous to withhold an immediate reply and say instead, "I'd like to discuss that with you next time." If you have been asked a question you honestly cannot answer, be glad. Admit you do not know the answer (this creates respect) *and then* promise: "I'll find out and let you know." Either way you have paved a second path to the householder's door for the RETURN CALL.

[11]Each congregation should produce a pamphlet for this purpose describing its location, phone number, services, beliefs, etc., and on the back containing a gospel presentation. The title of this may be "The_____ Church Invites You. . . ." The pamphlet should be slightly smaller than the colored insert that protrudes from it.

[12]See *infra.*

[13]See *infra.*

Throughout the visit, you have had in your hand the brochure "The _____ Church Invites" (hereafter designated "Tract"), with a "Can You Answer These Questions?" insert (hereafter designated "Insert") inside. You have *not* yet handed it to the householder. Now is the time to do so— but only after an explanation something like that which follows:

I've enjoyed our visit, but I promised not to take much of your time, so I should be going now. Before I do, however, I'd like to leave a couple of pieces of literature with you. This one (holding up the Tract) tells a little bit more about our Church. On the back it has some of the Bible verses about which I have been speaking in case you should care to look them up for yourself. This other piece (removing the colorful Inset for the first time— the surprise element creates new interest), explains about a free 6-week Home Bible Study course that we offer without obligation. (Here hand them both to the householder. Immediately reach into your briefcase, large handbag, etc., and for the first time produce the attractive H.B.S. *Workbook*). As the insert says, the course includes private instruction in your own home and free workbooks like this (holding it up, but *not* passing it over to the householder to look at closely. Put it away quickly and proceed.) I am sure you'll want to take time to read this material and talk it over with your husband/wife (or together) before you decide. Would this same hour next Tuesday be the best time for me to drop in and find out what you've decided? (*Assume* that you are coming back. Put the stress on *WHEN* you may do so. Be sure to settle upon a definite day and hour. With a very brief pleasantry of some sort leave as soon as possible. When you get into your car be sure to record the exact time arranged for the Return Call in the appropriate place on the V-card, with an initial evaluation. Pray silently for God's continued blessing upon your visit. Do not be discouraged if you are not always able to arrange for a Return Call. But be sure that you have made every legitimate effort to do so. Commit the household to God in prayer. Do not give up easily. *The Return Call is crucial for future contact.)*

Making the return call. Entering this time should be easy. You already know the householder and an appointment has been made. However, you may find that sometimes the householder has forgotten about it. Don't let this disturb you. If he is not home, leave a note and cheerfully call again as soon as possible. (Do all that you can to relieve him of any embarrassment this may have caused.) Other exigencies may be handled by the principle set forth earlier.

The twofold purpose of the Return Call is: (1) to talk further about salvation in Christ — but again only as fully as you sense would be appropriate; (2) to arrange for a H.B.S. Make this your fundamental aim, for whenever a H.B.S. is set up it provides at least six additional opportunities to speak about Christ. Discussion of the H.B.S. flows naturally from a question about the literature that you left on the first visit: "What did you think of the pamphlets I left? There were some rather interesting questions on this insert, weren't there?" It would be wise to carry additional copies in case your householder has lost or misplaced or thrown his away. Assume that he has read it, but keep him from the embarrassment of having to admit that he didn't. You may do this by immediately reading some of the questions on the Insert to "refresh" his mind, *before* you allow him to answer your question.

If it appears that it will be possible to establish a H.B.S., it is probably wise to do so immediately (again by arranging for a definite time and date) and departing as soon as possible.

Where the householder appears hesitant, encourage him by stressing additional advantages of such a study and by disclosing new facts. It may even be advisable at this point to take out the Workbook once more and point out a section or two in the first or second lesson that you think may arouse interest. Think positively: assume that he will agree to a H.B.S. After additional discussion, make what the salesman calls a second "close." Ask *when* (not whether) he would like to have the H.B.S. Successful salesmen know that objections are not always real and that people often like to be "sold" and sometimes need help in making good decisions. Offer all the genuine help and encouragement you can without employing questionable or unethical "hard sell" techniques.

If it appears that you are likely to receive a definite "no," try two more approaches: (1) Attempt to forestall that kind of a "no" by suggesting that perhaps the householder is not yet fully prepared to make a decision and should take another week or so to decide (and possibly to talk it over with another person). You may even suggest leaving the H.B.S. Workbook for a week so that the family may glance over it. (Indicate, of course, that you will return to pick it up. This will give you—like the Fuller Brush man—another reason for coming again at a time when it is possible that the householder will be in a different frame of mind.) (2) If that approach and all others fail, stay as long as is polite and present the gospel again as fully as possible with an exhortation to believe.

Once a H.B.S. date and time is arranged, *immediately* contact your team captain and/or the H.B.S. teacher and give him (them) all pertinent information. The teacher should immediately send a personal letter (or phone the householder) confirming the time and place and introducing himself by name. The letter is often more effective, because it does not give as ready an opportunity as the phone for a change of mind. The first day of the study, the visitor who arranged the study should accompany and introduce the teacher.

> Note: This manual should be used in conjunction with the rest of the materials in the Visitation Evangelism Packet. This method depends upon the functioning of the entire program as a unit. The manual should be given out at the time of instruction and demonstration of techniques, as provided for in the *Leader's Manual.* Discussion of questions and problems in necessary as well.

The Teacher's Guide

The Teacher's Guide to the *Workbook* and teaching of the Home Bible Study Course, *Cardinal Doctrines.*

Preparation

A. The teacher should read the ENTIRE course through, looking up all references, studying and understanding their relationship to the doctrine under discussion and underlining them in his Bible.
B. The teacher should fill in all correct answers to study assignments in his copy of the *Workbook.*
C. The teacher should make any necessary notes on his copy of the *Workbook.*
D. The teacher should pray for his students daily.

Teaching

A. The teaching period ordinarily should be one hour long. Make this a rule of thumb. With a peculiarly responsive group, perhaps 1½ hours will be better.
B. This hour should be divided into three parts:
1. Fifteen minutes for reading and discussing the answers to last week's assignment. The first week this time may be used to explain the *Workbook* and its use.
2. Twenty minutes teaching this week's lesson.

3. Twenty-five minutes' discussion of the lesson. (The last two items may vary according to the circumstances, but ample time should be given to both teaching and discussion.)

Particular Points to Stress

A. SALVATION. Every lesson has within it opportunities to stress salvation. Note these and use them. Thus there are a number of built in opportunities to lead the student to faith in Christ somewhere during the series of studies. The answer to the third question in the first lesson, and the concluding questions in the sixth lesson are designed to help you determine whether the student has yet come to faith in Christ. The length of the discussion period (among other things) is arranged to give opportunity to engage the student in personal discussion about his salvation.

B. BAPTISM. While taking care to emphasize that baptism does not save, unbaptized persons who become converts should be urged to obey the scriptural injunction to be baptized.

C. CHURCH MEMBERSHIP. The series of studies should begin without mention of this matter. As it progresses, however, and the teacher begins to win confidence, the *Workbook* raises the question in the fifth (the next to last) week. At this point, and not before, the matter of Liberalism and the challenge of biblical Christianity should be presented. The questions to be answered on the sixth week also raise the discussion. During the last two weeks your students may be invited to attend your church services, if they have not done so previously.

D. SPECIAL PROBLEMS. Matters of special concern to the householder that lie within the scope of the *Cardinal Doctrines* course, should be discussed if the student raises them. Matters beyond this scope should be deferred to a later time, when they can be considered in a second course. The teacher can help create lasting interest if he confines his discussion to the *Cardinal Doctrines,* always indicating that there will be opportunity to discuss these other matters after the course is completed. The doctrinal material given is minimal and looks forward to much more in greater depth at a later point.

Miscellaneous

If questions are asked that the teacher cannot answer, he should admit it honestly, and promise to find out the answer for next week. If he cannot obtain the answer on his own, he should contact his elder or his pastor about it. It is always wrong to try to "cover up" by giving some conjecture for an answer. The student will have more respect for the honest teacher. In teaching, explain everything; assume nothing. But do not move too rapidly in seeking to convert members; no one can believe until God has made him ready. Your responsibility is to present the gospel plainly and persuasively; it is God's part to work faith in him.

H.B.S. literature, left on the first visit, should be discussed, and during the return call seek to schedule a time and place for the beginning of a H.B.S. This should be attempted whether the householder has professed faith in Christ or not. The visitor should be prepared to commit the H.B.S. teacher to a definite date and time for the beginning of the class. This calls for prearrangement and subsequent contact with the teacher. If a H.B.S. is refused, try to arrange for another Return Call. Where it is possible, H.B.S. courses may be given for several families in a neighborhood at the same time in a conveniently located home.

The Program in Brief

1. INITIAL VISIT — Short gospel explanation (unless obvious opportunity for witness in depth is available), arrange definite time and place for return call; leave publicity and H.B.S. literature ("I shall return to discuss this with you when you have had an opportunity to read it").
2. RETURN CALL — Longer visit; discuss need for and way of salvation in depth. Mention H.B.S. literature; arrange definite time and date for H.B.S.
3. HOME BIBLE STUDY — A six-week course in the *Cardinal Doctrines of Christianity*. They are: The Doctrine of Scripture, God, Man, Salvation, Church, Future.

N.B. You can see that this program does not call for surveys or a mere invitation to attend the ＿＿＿＿ Church. Nor does it seek to win souls to Christ, then leave them. It endeavors to fulfill both of Christ's commands in Matthew 28 and thus avoid the pitfalls of many systems. APART FROM A DETERMINED EFFORT TO FOLLOW *BOTH*

PARTS OF THE PLAN, IT WILL BE FOUND INEFFECTIVE. A fundamental thesis is that it takes time and instruction to win men to Christ and to establish them firmly in the faith. Workers must count the cost.

SECONDARY APPROACHES

It was said earlier that the Visitation Evangelism campaign was a unit. No parts were to be dropped from it. Yet, this does not mean that other Home Bible study programs cannot be effective. One simple, straightforward method that has proved successful in actual experience is for members to invite friends and neighbors to a projected Bible study at their home. This can often be conducted in a very congenial atmosphere over coffee and doughnuts. Sometimes it is wise to relax the one hour rule under these circumstances.

Unchurched parents of Sunday School or Vacation Bible School pupils (or Pioneer Girls or Boys' Brigade) also may be invited to a Home Bible Study. In the course of extending the invitation to participate you may suggest: "We know your child is learning a good bit about the Bible at Sunday School (V.B.S.). Undoubtedly he will have questions. He may have asked you some real stumpers already. Some of these questions will be along these lines (hand the *Insert* to the parent). We think that it is important to help parents to know the answers to these questions so that home and church together can influence Johnnie in the right direction. So our church is offering a Home Bible Study Course for parents ...."

If fall and spring V.E. - H.B.S. campaigns are scheduled, it may be well to use the secondary approaches during the winter when it is difficult to visit door-to-door. And members of the congregation or the minister may also use the Home Bible Study program to a wide variety of particular needs and opportunities available to your congregation. Be creative.

The Student's Workbook

First Week: THE DOCTRINE OF THE SCRIPTURES

A. Revelation ("uncovering")
  1. For men to know God, He must reveal Himself.
  2. He has done so in two ways:
    a. *General Revelation*—through creation (Psalm 19:1-6). Creation reveals to all men that there is a Creator, and that we are sinners against Him without excuse (Romans 1:20), but does not tell us how to be freed from sin. Sin blinds men to the message of general revelation (I Cor.22), so we need—
    b. *Special Revelation*—through the Bible (Psalm 19:7-11). The "law." (Scripture) imparts truth that can "convert the soul" (v. 7). See also 2 Timothy 3:15. It contains "all things that pertain to life and godliness" (2 Peter 1:3), so that Christians may be "thoroughly furnished unto every good work" (2 Timothy 3:17). General revelation may be understood only through special revelation.
B. The Bible (this word means "book")
  1. Is inspired in the original Hebrew and Greek languages (Old and New Testaments respectively).
    a. "Inspired" means "God-breathed" (2 Timothy 3:17). This means its words are as truly God's as if He actually breathed them out in audible speech.
    b. Note: the writers were "moved" (2 Peter 1:21) and their writings "inspired."
    c. The Bible is the inspired words of God given through men.
    d. Inspiration assures us that the Bible is true and inerrant (cf. Psalm 119:140).
  2. The Bible is the standard of faith and practice. That means it is the rule by which we determine what to believe and do.
  3. Scores of prophecies, given hundreds of years before an event concerning minute details, and fulfilled exactly, confirm the truth that the Bible is from God. Here are three examples: cf. Micah 5:2 with Matthew 2:1; Zechariah 9:9 with Matthew 21:1-5; Psalm 22:16 with Luke 23:33, John 20:25, Zechariah 12:10.[1]

---

[1]Other passages for study night include Genesis 49:10; Psalm 2; 22:7,8,18,27; 110:1-Zacheriah 12:10; Daniel 9:24-27.

STUDY ASSIGNMENT *This Week:* Study 2 Timothy 3:15-17 and list
four ways in which Scripture is profitable
1......................... 2.......................... 3......................... 4........................
Consider: Have YOU been made "wise unto salvation"? Yes..... No.....
Next Week: List any questions you wish to ask. Make it a rule to study
part of the Bible every day, beginning with the gospel of John, then
Romans, then Acts, then Galatians, then Luke, then the rest of the
New Testament.

Second Week: THE DOCTRINE OF GOD

A. The Existence of God and Atheism.
   1. An atheist is literally "one without God," but popularly it means "one
who says there is no God."
   2. God's estimate of an atheist: Psalm 14:1.
      a. God never makes charges lightly, without reasons.
      b. A fool speaks beyond his knowledge. No one knows enough to say
there is no God. To say there is no God, one must be capable of being
everywhere at the same time. Otherwise God may be where he is not. To
do this one would have to *be* God. A fool speaks against all the evidence
(fulfilled prophecy, abundant testimony, the Bible, etc.).
B. The Knowledge of God and Agnosticism (literally, "ignorance")
   1. Two kinds of doubters: honest and dishonest.
   2. Dishonest men enjoy their doubts; honest men are pained by them.
The latter are really seekers to whom God will give the truth (John 7:17).
C. The Nature of God and Theism (belief in God)
   1. It is not enough to "believe in God" (James 2:19). It must be the true
God.
   2. Kinds of theism people believe in:
      a. Polytheism ("many gods")—Greeks, Romans, Mormons.
      b. Pantheism ("God is all")—Buddhism, Christian Science.
      c. Unitarianism ("one God")—Jews, Mohammedans.
      d. Trinitarianism ("one God Who is three Persons: Father, Son and
Holy Spirit")—Christians.
   3. As Father God planned salvation; as Son He came to earth to effect it;
as Spirit He applies it to individuals.
D. The Attributes of God.
   1. God is a Spirit (John 4:24)—A spirit is a person without a body.

2. God is infinite ("no bounds")—Psalm 147:5.

   a. As to presence—omnipresent ("present everywhere at once").

   b. As to knowledge—omniscient ("all-knowing").

   c. As to power—omnipotent ("all-powerful"—God can do anything He wants to do).

3. God is eternal—always has been and always will exist (Psalm 90:2).

4. God is immutable ("unchangeable")—James 1:17.

   a. As to person—love, mercy, justice, holiness, wrath.

   b. As to purpose—promises and commands remain the same.

5. God is Sovereign—everything is under His control and happens according to His purpose.

STUDY ASSIGNMENT *This Week:* Study Matthew 28:19, 2 Corinthians 13:14 and Titus 1:4. It would be blasphemous for the names of any persons less than equals thus to be linked with God, the Father. How do Acts 5:3,4 prove the Holy Spirit is God?

....

Next Week: Study Genesis 2:7. Of what two elements was man made?........
and.........According to Genesis 3:1-21, what happened to man?........
.... How does this affect us?...............

Third Week: THE DOCTRINE OF MAN

A Man Before the Fall.

1. Creation of—created "very good" (Genesis 1:31) in God's "image" (Genesis 1:26)—this image is not physical, because God has no body, but spiritual, intellectual and moral (cf. Colossians 3:10; Ephesians 4:24).

2. Nature of: Man has a physical and non-physical element (Genesis 2:7 James 2:26); Man IS a soul; HAS a body.

3. Duties of: To glorify God (Revelation 4:11); rule over the earth (Genesis 1:26); beget children (Genesis 1:28); work (Genesis 2:15—but no *labor* until fall).

B. Man After the Fall.

1. Consequences—shame (Genesis 3:7, 3:10); separation (Genesis 3:8) sentence of death (Genesis 2:17).

2. Life and Death Summarized are:

	LIFE (union)	DEATH (separation)
Physical	Body + Soul	Body — Soul
Spiritual	Soul + God (1 John 5:20; Romans 6:11)	Soul — God (Genesis 2:17; Ephesians 2:1)
Eternal	Body + Soul + God (John 5:24,25; 1 Thessalonians 4:13-17)	Body + Soul — God (Revelation 20:14; 2 Thessalonians 1:9)

All have physical life; all who have spiritual life will have eternal life too. Do you have spiritual life? eternal life?

C. Sin is fundamentally "lawlessness" (I John 3:4)

1. Two aspects: original sin. All are born with a sinful nature (Psalm 51:5; Romans 5:12) Adam's representative act brought guilt and corruption upon all; actual sin (Romans 3:23).

2. Two ways of sinning: doing what the law prohibits; not doing what the law commands.

3. Forgiveness of sin.

a. Sin is rebellion against God (Psalm 51:4), and therefore forgiveness must come from Him.

b. Forgiveness is through Christ alone (Ephesians 1:7).

c. This forgiveness comes when a sinner puts faith in Christ as Savior (Acts 26:18).

STUDY ASSIGNMENT *This Week:* Do you consider yourself a sinner? ....Study Revelation 21:27. Do you think your sins would defile heaven, and keep you from going there unless forgiven? Yes........ No........ Are they forgiven? Yes........ No........ *Next Week:* Read Matthew 27:24-54. Why did Christ die?..

Fourth Week: THE DOCTRINE OF SALVATION

A. Need for salvation. Last week's study showed how sin keeps men from heaven, and sends them to eternal death in hell. This is man's dilemma: How to be saved ("rescued") from hell to go to heaven. Salvation is from sin and its consequences.

B. False ways of salvation (Proverbs 14:12):

1. Good works (trying to do the best you can, or attempting to keep the Ten Commandments, etc.) Ephesians 2:8,9.

2. Water baptism (or other outward ceremonies): 1 Peter 3:21 makes it clear that it is the internal reality and not the external ritual that saves.

C. Salvation from sin by Christ alone:

1. Christ came to save sinners (I Timothy 1:15): God takes the initiative in salvation.

2. Salvation by faith in Christ—in His substitutionary and penal death for our sins (1 Peter 2:24) and His bodily resurrection from the dead (I Cor. 15:3).

D. Salvation has three phases (whoever has been justified is now being sanctified and at death will be glorified).

JUSTIFICATION (a past act)	SANCTIFICATION (a present process)	GLORIFICATION (a prospective act)
We have been saved	are being saved	will be saved
from the penalty of sin	the power of sin	the presence of sin

E. Assurance of Salvation. God would be a heartless Father, if He failed to let His children know they were His. He wants us to know it when we are saved (1 John 5:11). We know, because He has gone on record in the Bible. It is not arrogant to say you *know* you will go to heaven, because this salvation is Christ's work, not yours.

F. Permanence of Salvation. There are only two places where anything could go wrong with salvation: with the inheritance or the heir. But God has protected both (1 Peter 1:3-5). See also Romans 8:35-39; John 10:28 29: 17:12. Once saved, one can never be lost, God sees to it that all who are saved persevere to the end.

STUDY ASSIGNMENT *This Week:* Have you been saved? Yes...... No... Uncertain..... Do good works have anything at al to do with getting to heaven? Do they help? Yes..... No..... Why?.... .... Why is it not pre sumptuous for a Christian to say he knows he is saved?..................... ....If when once saved, we can never be los can we then sin as we please? .... *Next Week:* Read Matthew 16:18. What church is this?

Fifth Week: THE DOCTRINE OF THE CHURCH

A. Meaning of the word "church" (in the Bible this word never refers to a building).

   1. The Greek word means "assembly of called out ones."

   2. The church is God's people whom He has called out from the world to transact His business.

B. The Church has two aspects: Invisibility and Visibility.

   1. Invisible Church—is the body of Christ; composed of all who have been saved. There is no salvation outside of it (cf. Ephesians 5:23-27).

   2. Visible Church—mirrors the invisible; though membership is not necessary for salvation, God commands membership in it (Hebrews 13:7; 10:25). Composed of all who make a profession of faith and their children.

C. The Organization of the Church.

   1. Christ is Head. He exercises His lordship through men whom the Bible terms "elders." "Elder" occurs over 100 times in the Old Testament (see Numbers 11:16; I Samuel 8:4,5; Ezra 10:8). In the New Testament: Luke 22:66; I Timothy 3:1-7; 5:17; Titus 1:5-7; and Acts 20:17,28. "Elder" and "bishop" are used synonymously in the last two references. "Elder" speaks of his qualifications—maturity in the faith. "Bishop" speaks of his work (it means "overseer").

   2. Congregations were not independent. They were bound together, and elders from the churches made decisions that affected the whole church (Acts 15:6; 16:4,5).

D. Not all churches teach the truth (II Peter 2:1,2).

   1. Christ and the apostles predicted false teachers would come into the visible church (Matthew 24:11; Acts 20:29,30).

   2. Christians should separate from them (II Corinthians 6:14-7:1; I Timothy 6:5), as the apostles separated from paganism and the apostate Jewish church of their day.

E. Sacraments,

   1. Water baptism—commanded by Christ (Matthew 28:19,20). By sprinkling or pouring (cf. Acts 1:5 with Acts 2:3,17,8,33 — where the mode that the word expresses is shown: "poured"); never by immersion. Water baptism pictures the inward baptism of the Holy Spirit who is poured upon those who are regenerated (Romans 8:9; I Cor. 12:13). It depicts union with Christ and all that this entails (Romans 6:3-5).

   2. The Lord's Supper—I Corinthians 11:23-27; a remembrance and a witness; not a sacrifice. Christ is present spiritually (not physically) to bless those who partake in faith.

STUDY ASSIGNMENT *This Week:* Are you a member of the invis-
                                    ible Church? Yes........ No........ Are you a
member of a Biblical church? Yes........ No........ If not, what should you
do? ....
Next Week: Read Luke 16:19-31, and consider what happens when we
die. Are you prepared to die? Yes........ No........

Sixth Week: THE DOCTRINE OF THE FUTURE

A. The Intermediate State (between death and resurrection of the body).
  1. Death—the separation of the spirit from the body (James 2:26).
  2. After death—conscious existence in joy or suffering (Luke 16:19-31).
  3. Believers go to be "with Christ" (Philippians 1:23), Who is in heaven
(Colossians 3:1). This is gain (Philippians 1:21).
B. Christ will return (Acts 1:11). This is called the "Second Coming of
Christ."
  1. His return is yet future.
  2. He is coming personally (Acts 1:11).
  3. At His return living Christians will be "changed" — their bodies will
become immortal and incorruptible— (I Corinthians 15:52) and "caught
up together" with dead Christians whose bodies will be raised (I Thessalonians 4:16).
  4. The time of this return is unknown (I Thessalonians 5:1).
  5. Unbelievers will receive the wrath of God (I Thessalonians 5:3-9;
II Thessalonians 1:6-10).
C. The Eternal State
  1. Christ will send some into everlasting punishment, and others into
everlasting life (Matthew 25:46).
  2. Compare also the following: John 14:2,3; Revelation 20:15; 21:4,5.
  3. Remember; Christ is the only way to heaven (John 4:6).

WHAT NEXT? It has been a privilege to meet and study God's
                          Word with you these six weeks. By this time you
should be able to answer the following questions. If you can't or if
you are not sure about any of them, ask your instructor. 1. Have you
been saved? This is the primary question. 2. Have you been baptized?
3. Do you belong to a Biblical church?

This booklet was presented to:

_____

By the _____ church

_____

The Visitation Materials

1. The Insert

CAN YOU ANSWER
THESE QUESTIONS?

What happens when we die?

What is the purpose of life?

Is the Bible full of mistakes?

Will the world be destroyed by missile
warfare?

What is God like?

Why did Jesus Christ die?

Is there a heaven or hell?

IF YOU CANNOT, YOU NEED TO STUDY
YOUR BIBLE.

Our Church is happy to offer you a six week course of instruction in the "Cardinal Doctrines of Christianity."

This informative Home Bible Study is free. It includes free workbooks and private, personal instruction in your own home. If you wish, you may invite your friends and neighbors to enroll and study with you.

2. Visitation Record Card (V-Card)

Front

V-CARD

FAMILY NAME_____ PHONE_____

ADDRESS _____

Husband's first name_____Wife's_____

Church affil._____	Children's names	ages
Territory_____		
District _____		

Date of INITIAL visit_____   Response (NH, G, P[1])_____

RETURN CALL arranged for: Date_____Time_____

H. B. S. arranged for: Date_____Time_____

EVALUATION:

Visitor's Name_____

Reverse

H. B. S. REPORT

Week	Attend.	Assgmnt.	Salv.	Other
1				
2				
3				
4				
5				
6				

BAPT.?_____CH. MBRSHP.?_____

COMMENTS:

Teacher_____

---

[1]NH = Not Home, G = Good, P = Poor.

APPENDIX B

CHECK LIST

TEN PROBLEMS PREVELANT IN CONSERVATIVE CHURCHES

1. Too many meetings; emphasis upon crowds; tears families apart.

2. Lack of biblical priorities; wrong view of church, what constitutes "God's work," etc.

3. Pastors trying to do work that the people should do, contrary to Ephesians 4:11,12.

4. Abstract and impractical use of the Scriptures in preaching, counseling, teaching and administration; people bored, frustrated in attempts to effect change.

5. Fear of the world (science, etc.); leading to a professionalism that sells the Scriptures short.

6. Failure to emphasize discipline, structure and scheduling; sloppiness.

7. Failure to exercise Church discipline; weakness.

8. Resistance to biblically-induced change; rebellion spreading.

9. Lack of fellowship among members; hunger and dissatisfaction.

10. Unresolved personal difficulties in families and among members; loss of joy.

Procedure:

a. Rate your Church on each problem. (Good, fair, poor)

b. Then ask, "What are we doing about these problems?" (answer: significant effort being made, little being done, nothing)

c. Determine what should be done about each.

d. Be sure to do all of this on paper. Check your results with your elders. You might first ask them to rate the church as you have before comparing results.

APPENDIX C
THE FIVE YEAR PLAN

In the following pages adequate space has been left to draw up five five-year plans. For each there is a Worksheet and a year-by-year Program Planner. Programs, for different churches, kept in this same place will prove valuable for future references when drawing up new ones.

Plan One

Worksheet

1. Items in the present church program that do not foster worship, edification or evangelism:

Item	Eliminate altogether (state reason why)	Alter or revise (state how)

II. Items missing from the present church program that would foster worship, edification or evangelism:

Item	How to introduce it (describe place in program and process for bringing about the change)	Difficulties likely to be encountered in making the change and how to overcome them

Program Planner

Five Year Plan

Years:____ to ____	Eliminate	Introduce	Record of actual outcome (yes, no, date)
Changes			
First Year			
Second Year			
Third Year			
Fourth Year			
Fifth Year			

Plan Two

Worksheet

I. Items in the present church program that do not foster worship, edification or evangelism:

Item	Eliminate altogether (state reason why)	Alter or revise (state how)

II. Items missing from the present church program that would foster worship, edification or evangelism:

Item	How to introduce it (describe place in program and process for bringing about the change)	Difficulties likely to be encountered in making the change and how to overcome them

Program Planner

Five Year Plan

Years:_____ to _____	Eliminate	Introduce	Record of actual outcome (yes, no, date)
Changes			
First Year			
Second Year			
Third Year			
Fourth Year			
Fifth Year			

Plan Three

Worksheet

I. Items in the present
church program that
do not foster worship,
edification or evangel-
ism:

Item	Eliminate altogether (state reason why)	Alter or revise (state how)

II. Items missing from the present church program that would foster worship, edification or evangelism:

Item	How to introduce it (describe place in program and process for bringing about the change)	Difficulties likely to be encountered in making the change and how to overcome them

Program Planner

Five Year Plan

	Eliminate	Introduce	Record of actual outcome (yes, no, date)
Years:_____ to _____			
Changes			
First Year			
Second Year			
Third Year			
Fourth Year			
Fifth Year			

Plan Four

Worksheet

I. Items in the present church program that do not foster worship, edification or evangelism:

Item	Eliminate altogether (state reason why)	Alter or revise (state how)

II. Items missing from the present church program that would foster worship, edification or evangelism:

Item	How to introduce it (describe place in program and process for bringing about the change)	Difficulties likely to be encountered in making the change and how to overcome them

Program Planner

Five Year Plan

Years:＿＿ to ＿＿	Eliminate	Introduce	Record of actual outcome (yes, no, date)
Changes			
First Year			
Second Year			
Third Year			
Fourth Year			
Fifth Year			

Plan Five

Worksheet

I. Items in the present church program that do not foster worship, edification or evangelism:

Item	Eliminate altogether (state reason why)	Alter or revise (state how)

II. Items missing from the present church program that would foster worship, edification or evangelism:

Item	How to introduce it (describe place in program and process for bringing about the change)	Difficulties likely to be encountered in making the change and how to overcome them

Program Planner

Five Year Plan

			Record of actual outcome (yes, no, date)
Years:____ to ____	Eliminate	Introduce	
Changes			
First Year			
Second Year			
Third Year			
Fourth Year			
Fifth Year